Malcolm Cooper and Kendall Christie

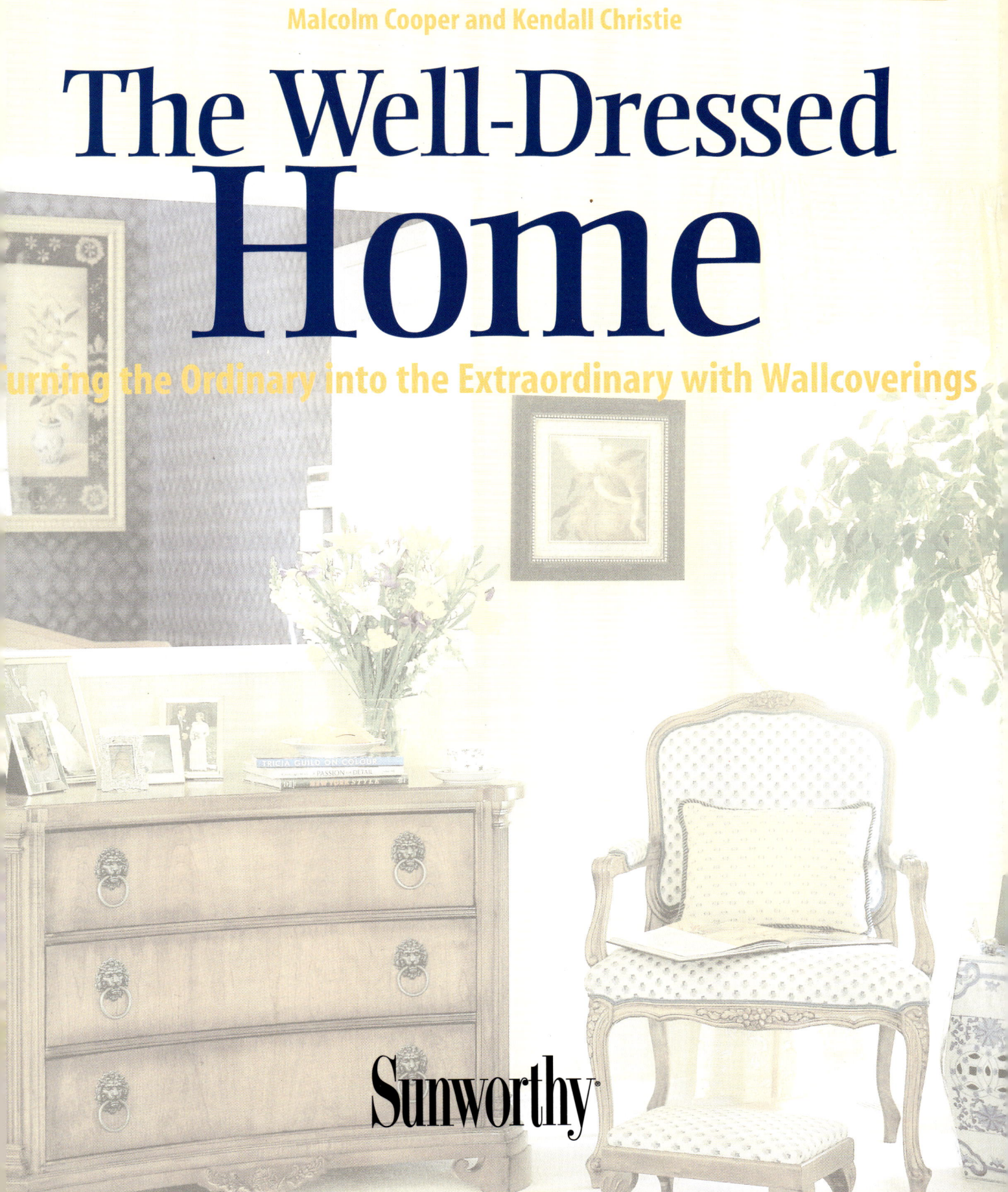

The Well-Dressed Home

Turning the Ordinary into the Extraordinary with Wallcoverings

Sunworthy

Copyright © 1998

Imperial Home Decor Group LLC
All rights reserved. No part of this publication may be reproduced or transmitted in any form or by any means, or stored in a data base and retrieval system, without the prior written permission of the publishers.

First published in 1998 by
Imperial Home Decor Group
23645 Mercantile Road
Cleveland, Ohio 44122

ISBN 0-9684081-0-9

Produced by
Publications-Plus Inc.
2330 Millrace Court, Unit 2
Mississauga, Ontario L5N 1W2

Printed and bound in Canada

Book Design:	Derek Chung
Photography:	Ted Yarwood
	front cover, pages 4, 5, 6, 8, 9, 10, 11, 24, 35, 36, 37, 38, 40, 42, 43 (before), 44, 46, 47, 48, 49 (before), 50, 51, 52, 53 (before), 54, 55, 56, 57, 58, 59, 60, 61, 62, 63, 64, 65 (before), 66, 68, 69, 70, 72, 73, 74, 75 (before), 77, back cover.
	Virginia Macdonald
	inside front cover; page 32; wallcovering/fabric samples: pages 43, 45, 49, 53, 57, 61, 65, 67, 71, 75, 76; inside back cover.
	IHDG
	pages 12, 14, 15, 17, 18, 21 and 23.
Illustrations:	Julian Cleva
Creative Consultant:	Malcolm Cooper
Project Manager:	Kendall Christie
Styling:	Suzanne Davison
	Interior Designs Inc.
Wallpapering:	Donald Miller Management Services Limited
Sewing of Window Coverings and Soft Furnishings:	Elisa Guido
	Mafalda Di Felice
House Provided By:	Country Homes
	Mayfield Village

Acknowledgments

It has been my great pleasure and enormous good fortune to have worked with a group of cooperative and talented professionals in decorating the *Well-Dressed Home* and in producing this book. At Imperial Home Decor Group, I am grateful to Tracey Paul, whose help was invaluable; to Duncan Campbell and Lori Davis, who provided constant support along with great editorial ideas; and especially to Julie McGregor, whose imagination and creativity took flight in "The Secret Garden" room. A special thank you to Malcolm Cooper, whose design and color expertise is always our inspiration.

Without the generosity of Country Homes contractors Ernie and Tony Rinomato and their staff, there would have been no home to dress. I thank them for lending us the new subdivision house, which they built, and for being patient and understanding throughout the life of the project.

At Sears Canada and Sears Whole Home, Dan Weir, Christine Hudson, Maureen Gallagher and their staff graciously lent us beautiful furniture and accessories with which to decorate the house. A special thank you to Emily Cohen and Gail Hamilton at McCalls Patterns for their enthusiastic support of our Sunworthy house project and for providing the sewing patterns; and to Elisa Guido and Mafalda DiFelice, who put their sewing machines in high gear to transform those patterns into the fabulous window coverings and bedding ensembles, which add so much to the house.

I thank contractor Don Miller and his staff for their dedication to the task of hanging the wallcoverings; and Sunworthy's Steve Paul, who came through at the last minute. My thanks, too, to Marie Christie, Lynda Craig and Annalisa DiFelice, who were always available to help.

A small clutch of enormously creative people collaborated on decorating and photographing our well-dressed home and I thank them warmly: interior designer Suzanne Davison and photographer Ted Yarwood and his assistants, Andrea Emard and Margaret Mulligan. My thanks, too, to graphic designer Derek Chung for making this book so beautiful.

It is with enormous gratitude that I thank my husband, David, and my son, Connor Ketcheson, who put up with far more than they should have, and my daughter, Emma, who delayed her arrival until almost the last minute and then showed patience and understanding far beyond her age!

Finally, my thanks to friends and co-workers at the Sunworthy Brand, whom I will miss.

To these and all the other people who have contributed in any way, my warmest thanks.

– K. Christie

Contents

INTRODUCTION 7

CHAPTER 1:
WALLCOVERINGS THROUGH THE YEARS 9
- Looking back: the history of wallcoverings 9
- Patterns and styles today 10

CHAPTER 2:
COLOR AND DESIGN 13
- The power of color 13
- Design basics 16

CHAPTER 3:
GET READY TO DECORATE 19
- Draw up a decorating plan 19
- Analyze your home 19
- Define the room uses 19
- Describe the look you love 20
- Choose a color scheme 20
- Make the rooms relate 20
- Decide where to begin 22

CHAPTER 4:
WALLCOVERING BASICS 25

- Types of wallcoverings 25
- Selecting the "right" wallcovering 27
- Wallcovering cleanups 27
- Calculating quantities 28
- Pattern-match repeats 30

CHAPTER 5:
READY, SET, GO! 33

- Prepare the surface 33
- Get the hang of hanging wallcoverings 35

CHAPTER 6:
THE WELL-DRESSED HOME 41

- Welcome home! 41
- Inviting entrance hall 43
- Sunny family/living room 45
- Distinctively dramatic dining room 49
- Sunny eating nook 53
- Perfectly practical powder room/ hideaway laundry 57
- Romantic retreat 61
- Suite retreat 65
- Double-duty den 67
- The secret garden 71
- Refreshing and relaxing bath 75
- More decorating ideas using wallcoverings 76

GLOSSARY 78
INDEX 80
SOURCES 80

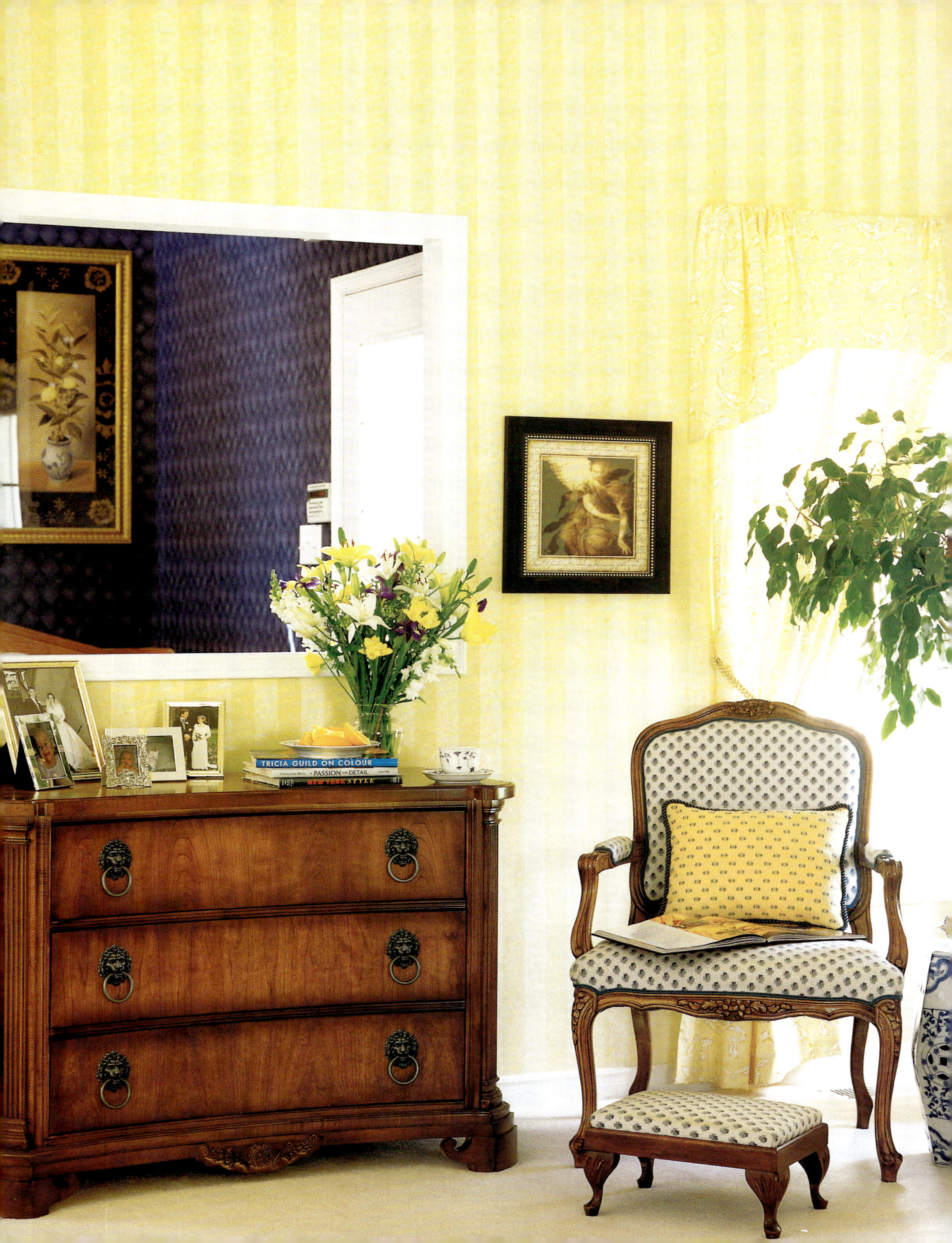
TRICIA GUILD ON COLOUR
PASSION FOR DETAIL
NEW YORK STYLE

Introduction

Wallcoverings offer an extensive array of decorating possibilities, introducing color and pattern — and more — into a home. With wallcoverings, you can brighten a room, lower a ceiling, frame a window, create a calm or bold interior, mask undesirable details or accent the highlights of a house. With wallcoverings, you can create illusions of another era, erect faux columns to embellish a doorway, turn a bare-box bedroom into a flower-strewn bower or fill a windowless room with light and pizzazz. Because wallcoverings are available in so many colors, textures, patterns and styles and are so easy to install, they have a place in every room in the house.

In the *Well-Dressed Home*, you'll find everything you need to know in order to decorate your home with wallcoverings: the types available today, how to calculate the amount to buy, how to prepare your surfaces and how to hang them. You'll find design hints, color theory, suggestions for selecting a color scheme and tips for tying your rooms together and coordinating your furnishings.

Then, you'll take a room-by-room tour of a house decorated from top to bottom with exciting new wallcoverings. While it is unlikely that you would cover all surfaces of a house with wallcoverings, this one brims with ideas from which to pick and choose. You'll see innovative faux-finish wallcoverings on doors, columns, wainscotting and walls. We'll show you how we transformed a little girl's room into an enchanting secret garden. You'll also find intricate all-new die-cut borders and pierced borders rimming ceilings and window boxes and combinations of coverings used as découpage. Our detailed instructions will inspire you to use wallcoverings to decorate your personal rooms. We'll even show you how to create decorative accessories that will make your house as pretty as a picture.

Hand-embossed leather, ca. 1710

CHAPTER 1

Wallcoverings Through the Years

LOOKING BACK: THE HISTORY OF WALLCOVERINGS

It's obvious that there's a real excitement about wallcoverings today. Houses are alive with them, while stores dedicated to selling them abound. The variety of colors, patterns and styles, availability and ease of use make wallcoverings a very popular choice.

It should be no surprise, however, that today's wallcoverings bear little resemblance to their earliest origins. After all, wall decorating dates back to the cave dwellers, who painted rudimentary, but realistic portrayals of daily events on the walls of their caves.

Fast-forward and you'll find more wall decorations during Egyptian, Greek and Roman times. These were more sophisticated and detailed, pictorial and patterned. All were applied directly to the walls. No hint of "wallpaper" appeared until 200 BC in China.

History contains no other record of wallpaper until the eighth century, when the Arabs introduced papermaking to Europe. Even then, paper's use as a wallcovering was not an immediate success. Wealthy Europeans preferred to hang woven materials and leather on their walls, both for esthetic and practical reasons: leather and fabrics were better insulators than paper against the damp and cold that prevailed in their poorly heated homes.

Tapestries, leather, wood panels and ceramic tiles continued to line the walls of the wealthy throughout the 15th and 16th centuries, although there is evidence that some hand-decorated wallpaper was used sparingly at this time. It was the invention of the printing press, however, that broadened the availability of wallpapering, and as the 17th century emerged, so did the wallpapering industry.

Not surprisingly, the earliest mass-produced patterns imitated fabrics, the process often resulting in "flocked" paper. A century later, pictorial paper panels appeared, which replicated original art painted on wood-paneled walls, but were affordable only to the aristocracy. Some of the designs were so complicated, they required as many as 3,000 wood blocks to produce the landscapes, town views, classical ruins and mythological scenes popular at the time. Printed on durable linen rag paper, a few have survived even to this day.

Toile de Jouy panoramic design, mid 19th century

The wallpaper industry changed radically in the mid-1800s with the introduction of machine printing

Machine interpretation of a block print, late 19th century

Pictorial design, late 19th century

Panel, late 19th century

Surface print, early 20th century

on paper — a faster and cheaper method that saw the price of wallpaper drop so considerably, it became available to the masses. The industry increased production, but design standards dropped; no longer were the beautiful patterns and fine details of hand-blocked papers for sale.

It was not until the early 20th century that an industry dedicated to producing well-executed innovative wallpapers revived. The silk-screening process popular in the 1930s made it all possible. Today's modern technology, driven by computers and fueled by advancements in pigments and materials, has taken wallcoverings to new heights of excellence in design and manufacturing standards, improving both the quality of wallcoverings and ease of handling.

PATTERNS AND STYLES TODAY

Because wallcoverings were first made to imitate tapestries, woven wallhangings and fine fabrics, some timeless patterns based on these early designs have retained their appeal to this day and are as elegant as they were centuries ago. Referred to as the **traditionals**, they include **damasks, orientals, crewel and documentary designs, such as toile de Jouy and paisley**. All of these patterns are perfect for decorating a home in a classic traditional manner.

Damask designs derive from damask fabric (a woven material with its pattern reversed on the underside), which was popular during the early 15th century. It is characterized by perfectly balanced motifs, such as acanthus leaves, forming the repeat pattern.

Oriental patterns imitate colors and designs found in the art of China and the Far East. Stylized birds and floral elements are favorite motifs.

Crewel designs, usually imitative of bold embroidery stitches, reflect English and East Indian renditions of the "tree of life" pattern.

Documentary designs are based on old paper or fabric documents. The best known are the **toile de Jouy** designs, named for the region in France where fabrics of this type were manufactured in the late 18th century. Toiles nearly always depict romantic pastoral landscapes populated with animals and people in period dress.

Paisley patterns have an historical background, too: their motifs are based on organic shapes that first appeared on fine woolen shawls woven in Kashmir in the 17th century.

Some early wallcoverings were made of actual materials, such as **grasscloth, burlap, linen, silk** and **wool**. They are still available but are now manufactured with a durable paper backing, which makes for easy application. Today, modern printing techniques have made it possible to replicate these real materials on either paper or vinyl, thus creating faux grasscloth and linen, etc. Likewise, simulated **wood grains, bricks, stucco** and **cork** are now possible and popular, because the cost of decorating with the wallcovering version is far less than with the real material.

Today's tastes have popularized the **geometrics** — stripes, plaids, polka dots and checks, as well as classic lattice, grille and tile designs. Contemporary demands for **faux finishes** have given rise to a proliferation of exciting wallcoverings replicating marble and other stones, while the popularity of the **country** look has seen a burst of patterns with coordinating country themes. **Florals** never lose their appeal: they simply change their "look" every decade or so, swinging from bold and bright to soft and muted. The newest styles in wallcoverings, which have enormous appeal for the contemporary decorator, are **novelty** patterns with motifs for use in kitchens, bathrooms and children's rooms — further proof that patterns exist to suit every taste.

The demand today may be responsible for launching new styles and patterns, but it's contemporary technology that has improved the quality of printing and reproduction and made possible such developments as die-cut borders, which are sculpted pierced and self-sticking, and Stick 'n' Play™ borders, which can be repositioned or removed. Both are easy to apply and finish off a room with flair. There has never been a better time to consider decorating with wallcoverings than right now!

Formal design with architectural influence, early 20th century

Surface print, early 20th century

Art Nouveau design, early 20th century

Red is a favorite color in dining areas because it stimulates the appetite. Here, it is most prominent in the dramatic fabrics that coordinate with the wallcovering borders.

CHAPTER 2

Color and Design

THE POWER OF COLOR

Since color is the basis for all decorating schemes, becoming "color smart" is vital! Understanding what color is, how colors affect you and how they relate to each other builds confidence in your ability to make wise decorating choices.

Explained scientifically, color is light, which is carried on wavelengths that the eye perceives and transmits to the brain. The brain processes this information so that you "see colors."

Objects are "colored" because of their pigments. Pigments absorb some *light* colors and reflect other *light* colors. An object that you see as blue in fact absorbs all the other *light* colors but blue *light*. This unabsorbed *light* is reflected onto the eye, and the brain "sees" it as blue.

Every discussion of color and the relationship of one color to another begins with the color wheel (see page 16), an arrangement of 12 colors in a circle in the order of the spectrum. (A rainbow in the sky exhibits the colors of the spectrum; so does light passing through a prism.)

Bold and Exciting

The color wheel sets related colors close to each other and complementary colors opposite each other, making the color wheel an important reference point when selecting a color scheme. Colors that fall opposite each other on the wheel (red and green; blue and orange; yellow and purple) are called complementary colors. When two complementary colors are viewed side by side, they intensify each other so that, for instance, red appears redder and green greener. For this reason, a decorating scheme based on complementary colors is bold and exciting.

Relaxing and welcoming

Adjoining colors (also called analogous colors) are those that exist next to each other on the color wheel. Decorating with adjoining colors produces a relaxing and welcoming ambience.

High-impact

Triad colors — three colors equidistant from each other on the color wheel — produce high-impact decorating schemes, particularly if one of the three colors is used predominantly and the other two play subordinate roles as accents.

Warm and cool colors

Colors are said to be "warm" or "cool." If you like to live in a cozy setting, wrapped in an ambience reminiscent

Pastel colors and small all-over patterns visually expand the size of a small room. The horizontal lines created by the border at ceiling height and the chair rail further create a sense of space.

Coordinating wallcoverings unify two rooms and define their separate uses. The plain faux texture of the dining room wallcovering gets a boost from the addition of dark stripes in the hallway. A border of colorful fruits ties the two spaces together.

of a summer day, you'd be wise to select a decorating scheme based on warm colors. If you prefer the calm that prevails in colors that lack sun-drenched touches, you'll be happiest in rooms decorated with cool colors.

Look again at the color wheel. Draw an imaginary line vertically through the middle. The cool receding colors fall to the left of this line. The warm advancing colors fall to the right. However, these are not absolutes, for there are "warm" reds and "cool" reds, depending on the amount of yellow the red contains (making it a "warm red") or the amount of blue it contains (making it a "cool" red). Any color can be made warmer by increasing its yellow content, while any color can be made cooler by increasing its blue content.

Colors look different in different lights. When contemplating a color to use in decorating, the light in which it is seen will greatly affect the way you perceive it. This is important to remember when picking wallcoverings in a store lit by fluorescent bulbs. Be sure to view samples of wallcoverings (or paints) in the rooms in which they will be used — both during the day and with the lights on at night, so that you get a true sense of how they will appear.

Colors arouse emotions

Colors have a real impact on how we behave and feel. This is partly a result of automatic behavioral responses to color. It is also partly due to learned responses influenced by age, sex, cultural background and other factors. This means your choice of colors will affect how comfortable you will be in your surroundings.

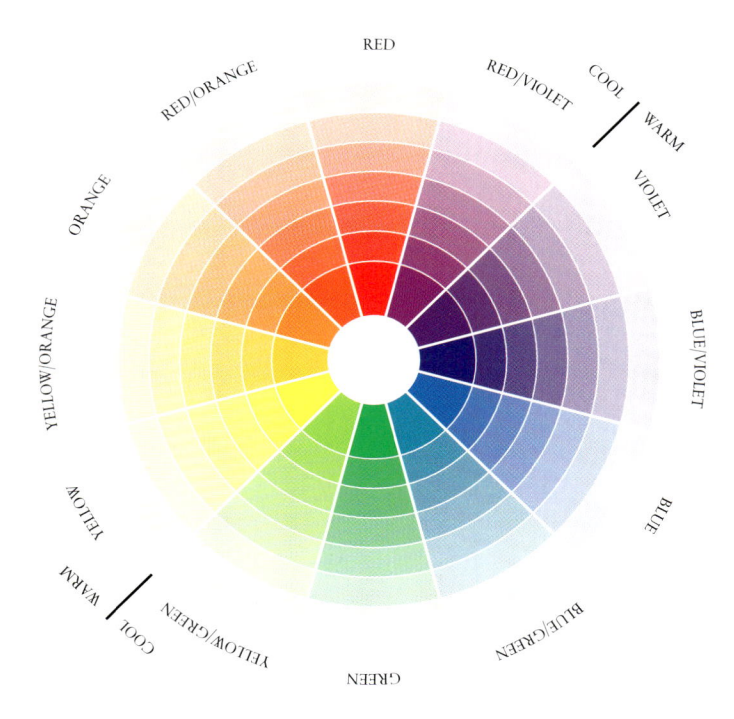

For example, green encourages feelings of emotional well-being; one feels tranquil and refreshed in green surroundings. Pale green tones are particularly soothing; they are an excellent color choice in a bedroom. Green's popularity is so universal, it is often considered a "neutral" color.

Red is a passionate color, perceived as aggressive, strong and vital. Because it stimulates the appetite, red is a favorite color for decorating dining rooms.

Yellow's popularity is easy to understand, for it reminds us of sunshine and warmth and is always uplifting and cheery.

Though viewed as utilitarian and earthy, brown has a subtle richness and is associated with comfort and warmth, making it a favorite decorating color.

Blue is a calming color you can enjoy forever without tiring of it. Blue is sometimes considered a "neutral" because of its enduring qualities and ability to partner with so many other colors.

Universally feminine and soothing, pink suggests innocence, softness and good health.

Purple, sophisticated, mysterious and perceived as "expensive," is known to settle emotions and suppress appetites, but it is a difficult color to live with in large amounts over long periods of time.

Easy-living white, associated with purity and truthfulness, comes in many shades, both "cool" and "warm," depending on its blue or yellow content.

Black, a distinctive, bold and classic color, is a great background shade for layering on other colors, though it can be oppressive in large amounts.

Your personality, your favorite "look," favorite colors and your individual rooms will all help you target the color family you'll select for decorating.

DESIGN BASICS

Entire books have been written on the subject of design principles, but knowing just a few will make you feel more comfortable when making decisions for your home.

If you are decorating a small room, keep in mind that light colors on walls and ceilings, as well as wallcoverings featuring small patterns on light colors set against light-colored backgrounds, will make a room appear larger than it really is. A light-colored carpet or bleached wood floor, and pale-colored lightweight window coverings further enhance the sense of spaciousness. Reflective surfaces, such as lacquered furniture and mirrors, also expand the apparent size of a small room. Paring down to a minimum of furniture and accessory pieces opens up a room, while low small-scale furniture creates a light open effect.

Large rooms, on the contrary, can be cozied up and reduced in perceived size if they are decorated in rich intense colors, using wallcoverings and window treatments with large patterns featuring warm colors. Rough textures on carpets and upholstery and large-scale furniture items in darker colors will fill empty cold spaces.

If ceilings are too high or too low, they can easily be brought into line: dark colors, such as deep blue or brown, used on a high ceiling will "lower" it. Similarly, light colors (or white) will "raise" a low ceiling.

Color is the key to "squaring up" long narrow rooms: simply decorate the short end walls in a dark warm color to bring them forward visually and decorate the long side walls in a light color, so that they will recede and seem farther apart.

When arranging furniture in any sized room, be sure to take traffic-flow patterns into account. You don't want to be bumping into a chair every time you pass through a room to get to the next one! Anchor the furniture arrangement with one large-scale piece, such as a sofa or armoire and, for balance, add other pieces with less weight and size. Be sure that the eye has interesting things to focus on, both high and low in the room: you need a variety of heights. Choose a focal point around which the furniture will be grouped, e.g., a fireplace, attractive built-ins for a television or sound system or a view out a window.

Finally, be sure to provide appropriate lighting. Rooms benefit from three types of lighting: general (overall ambient lighting); task (light directed onto small areas for such activities as reading or writing); and accent (to highlight desirable areas or create a mood) from wall-mounted sconces, for instance.

Sunshine colors brighten a kitchen and eating area. Common motifs appear in the wall-coverings in both spaces; accessories take their color cue from the flowers on the border.

Color and Design 17

Numerous patterns, all with animal-prints themes, appear on wallcoverings, borders, window treatments and accessories for a totally coordinated look that gives a room an energetic vitality.

CHAPTER 3

Get Ready to Decorate

DRAW UP A DECORATING PLAN

Starting a decorating scheme is often the hardest part of the task. Where should you begin?

Start by analyzing your home (its assets and liabilities) and the way you live in it. Then, define your desired style or "look" and choose a color scheme. The next step is to devise a comprehensive decorating plan and organize how you'll implement it. That's it in a nutshell! Here's how to do it in more detail.

ANALYZE YOUR HOME

Room by room, list the following:

- the assets (the room's best features, which you'll want to highlight)
- the liabilities (the room's problem areas, which you'll want to downplay or camouflage)
- the size
- the shape (square? long? L-shaped?)
- the windows (too many? too few? placed awkwardly? strangely proportioned?)
- the ceilings (too high? too low?)
- take special note of architectural features, such as fireplaces, mantels, moldings, pipes, ducts, radiators, etc.

In each room, you'll want to highlight the best features by drawing attention to them with wallcovering borders, coordinated designs or special paint colors and treatments that set them apart from the rest of the room. Similarly, you'll want to downplay problem zones by covering them with wallcovering that matches the walls, hiding them with decorative screens or planning built-ins to camouflage the offending items. For other specific design tips, see pages 16 and 17.

DEFINE THE ROOM USES

Ask yourself these three questions:

- what is the function of each room?
- does it get a lot of use?
- is it a high-traffic area?

The function of a room will influence the way you decorate it. You want to put your best face forward in a "public" room, such as a hallway, living or dining room. Colors should be warm and welcoming, the furnishings comfortable, the style or "look" exciting. In heavily used areas, such as a family room, kitchen or hallway, durability must also be considered, dictating washable wear-friendly wallcoverings and sturdy stain-resistant fabrics.

In getaway rooms, such as bedrooms, bathrooms, dens and home offices, you can relax a little in your choice of fabrics and wallcoverings, because they will be less exposed to wear and tear than in other areas of the house.

DESCRIBE THE LOOK YOU LOVE

Ask yourself these questions:

- are you attracted to contemporary styles, country themes, traditional looks or eclectic mixes?
- is your lifestyle casual or formal?

For some people, defining the look they love is difficult. The choices are many and complicated by the fact that, today, the lines between styles are not drawn as rigidly as they once were. This is evident in the popularity of eclectic-style decorating, which incorporates furnishings that span many periods and "looks."

The best way to establish a style preference is to cut out magazine pictures of rooms and furnishings that you find appealing and file them together in a folder or binder. Collect color samples, wallcovering and fabric swatches. Soon, you'll see a trend emerge, as your "ideas file" reveals repeated patterns, colors and styles of decorating.

Your lifestyle is also a consideration. If you are a casual person and like to "put your feet up," you'll want to decorate in a way where comfort and ease are paramount. If, on the other hand, you are a more traditional person and like things to be orderly and formal, you'll likely be most happy in an environment that is upscale and elegant, sophisticated and balanced.

CHOOSE A COLOR SCHEME

Everybody has favorite colors and color combinations, but many people don't know what they like. Look analytically at your wardrobe and you'll see colors you obviously like — since you choose to wear them! Some of your clothing — a scarf or tie, for instance — likely has patterns incorporating several colors. Look at how well these colors go together, and you'll get an idea of how to select your multicolored palette for decorating. Successful decorating schemes work well when they use a maximum of three colors. One should be the main color (used on the walls or for window treatments or carpeting, since these are the biggest surfaces to decorate); the other one or two colors should be used in smaller amounts as accents. Many patterned fabrics and wallcoverings make choosing a color scheme easy because they contain a good combination of colors, which you can see at a glance work well together. Wallcovering books are particularly useful because the coordinating patterns are presented side by side in sample books.

In an appealingly decorated room, fabrics and wallcoverings do not contain more than three or (at most) four different patterns; they also have common elements, such as motifs and colors. You can create a dynamic space by combining stripes, plaids or checks and floral, in both small- and large-scale patterns, as long as there are some solid areas in one of the colors to provide balance.

MAKE THE ROOMS RELATE

In decorating a house where rooms lead off an entrance hall — or in an apartment where rooms lead off one another or can be viewed from a central point — it is essential to formulate a decorating plan for all the rooms. Even if they will not be redecorated at one time, they need to be linked from a design sense, using colors or patterns that will appear, in some form, in all the rooms. Individual rooms, such as a kitchen, child's bedroom, den or a bathroom, may be decorated in any style without giving thought to their neighboring spaces, if they are out of view of the main entrance.

The hallway gives the first impression of a house or apartment, so this is a natural place to start a scheme. Since you have already collected samples and pictures, you now know the "look" you want to create and the elements required to achieve it. Choosing a wallcovering to suit that style is easy because the titles of wallcovering books will lead you to patterns that represent particular styles.

Successfully decorated hallways often incorporate designs that are "balanced", e.g., a patterned stripe, damask, simple geometric or even the textured effect of linen or grasscloth.

The bold wallcovering in the inviting entrance hall welcomes visitors warmly. The border detail reappears in rooms that lead off the hall.

The next room encountered is usually the living room. Here, it is best to have a restful design on the walls, rather than one that is busy and overwhelmingly bold. How do you relate the living room to the entrance hall? One way is to creatively mix a linen-look wallcovering in the hall with a color-coordinated toile de Jouy, for example, in the living room — or the reverse — thus tying the two rooms together without using the exact same wallcovering. You can use these same coordinating patterns in fabrics for window coverings, upholstery and cushions to further link the two rooms together.

In many of today's homes, condominiums and apartments, the L-shape living/dining room is a standard feature. While the wall treatments in these areas should relate to each other, it is not necessary to limit yourself to one pattern. A coordinating wallcovering will visually define the rooms; they are easy to select because coordinating coverings are shown together in sample books. Table runners, placemats and dining chairs sewn and upholstered from fabric that coordinates with the living room wallcovering will further unify the room.

In homes with a separate dining room, wallcoverings can be totally different in mood and color from those in the living room, but should relate in some way to the hallway. You can create a traditional look with a wallcovering-border chair rail that divides the wall horizontally and features different (but coordinating) wallcovering patterns above and below the "rail." Or you could use handsome damasks or simple documentaries, which decorate traditional dining rooms with panache. If a contemporary dining room is your choice, look for a striped, geometric or sophisticated faux-finish wallcovering pattern.

Kitchens have emerged as one of the most stylishly and boldly decorated rooms, thanks to the vast number of scrubbable wallcoverings available today. The choice of the design is usually determined by the style of the cabinetry in the room. Kitchen-theme motifs (fruits, vegetables and natural designs, such as plants, leaves, botanicals) and linen-looks are all colorful and interesting choices.

These same scrubbable wallcoverings mean that bathrooms can look as luxe and lively as the rest of the house. Because you don't spend a lot of time in these rooms, it is here that decorating rules can be overlooked. This is particularly true in small powder rooms, where large-scale designs can create tremendous impact — especially if the wallcoverings are applied to the ceiling as well as the walls and if the window coverings are sewn in matching fabric. If you feel compelled to tie in these rooms with the hallway or adjoining room, consider painting their baseboards and trim in the same color.

Bedrooms are places for relaxing as well as sleeping, so the right mood is very important here. You can choose a color that you have used elsewhere in the house, even as an accent, or one that has appeared in a pattern. In the bedroom, patterns should be cool, restful and fairly simple — neither overwhelming nor frenetically busy. Blues and greens, yellows and pinks, clean open florals, paisleys, simple stripes or plaids, traditional chintzes or documentaries are all good choices for the bedroom.

Other rooms, such as a study, guest room, sewing room or den/office, are places where you can be bold and experimental! Patterns can be mixed and matched on walls and ceilings. Foliage designs can bring the outside in, along with wicker, bamboo, cane or trellis designs.

DECIDE WHERE TO BEGIN

If you are starting from scratch, with no furnishings or hard-to-change features, you are lucky! Here's your opportunity to follow the suggestions, above, and map out a color and pattern scheme that will take you through to the end of your decorating project, even if you intend to do a few rooms now and the rest later. If you want to entertain your friends as soon as possible and get settled in a comfortable living and dining room, then you should begin to decorate in these two rooms first. If, on the other hand, comfort in your bedroom is of paramount importance, you should start there. The choice is yours.

If you are redecorating and already have many elements firmly in place, the task of selecting colors and wallcoverings is a little harder because you'll need to take into account and work with existing furniture, carpets, appliances, plumbing fixtures, etc.

Perceived as sophisticated, purple appears as both a main color and as an accent shade in a pretty floral bathroom.

Can you stand to live with your carpets for a few more years until you can afford to replace them? Or should you do it now because they are such a dominant feature? You'll have to decide what you plan to keep, what you'd like to replace — and when.

Whatever your situation, you are now armed with information, feeling confident and ready to put it all together.

WISE ADVICE FROM THE PROS

- Gather all your tools and supplies before you start. Make sure you have enough of everything.

- Read all product labels and manufacturers' instructions carefully.

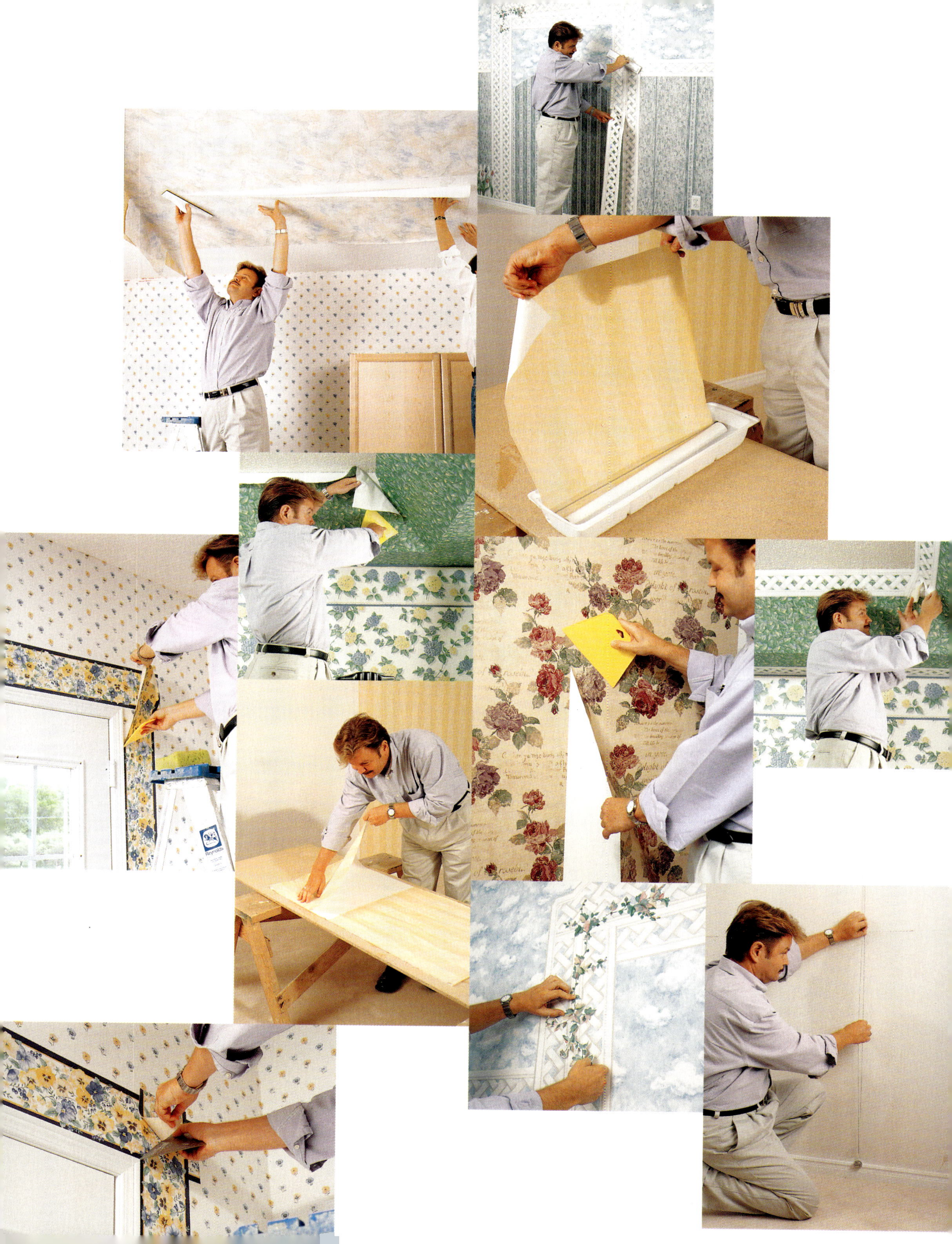

CHAPTER 4

Wallcovering Basics

TYPES OF WALLCOVERINGS

Until recently, the word "wallpaper" was used to describe a decorative covering applied to walls, because most of the coverings were made from paper. Today, however, the word "wallcovering" is more accurate, because vinyls and natural materials, such as silk, grasscloth, linen and even wool, are used for decorating walls and, indeed, other surfaces.

Most wallcoverings are prepasted, so that they adhere to the wall after they have been immersed for a brief period in a tray of water. This enables you to easily do it yourself. In some cases, wallcoverings still need special paste and treatment before hanging. The manufacturer's instructions on wallcovering rolls specify how they should be attached to the wall: be sure to read them carefully.

Wallcoverings are grouped into the following categories:

TYPE: Strippable vinyl coat

Characteristics: Paper substrate is printed, then sprayed with vinyl. It is usually prepasted. It is called "strippable" because it can be dry-stripped from the wall, if applied according to the manufacturer's instructions.

Benefits: Print quality of design is excellent; it's easy to hang and remove; vinyl-coated surface provides washability and is fairly durable.

Areas of use: All areas; good in areas of moderate moisture.

Removal hints: If properly applied, strip off, then wash the wall with mild detergent. If improperly applied (additional adhesive used or walls not properly prepared), etch or score the vinyl coating with a coarse sandpaper or etching tool. Apply a wallcovering-remover solution. Allow to soak in for 15 minutes, then use a wall scraper to remove the wallcovering. Several applications may be required.

TYPE: Paper-backed vinyl or solid vinyl

Characteristics: Solid vinyl layer is laminated or bonded to a paper backing sheet.

Benefits: Durable, scrubbable and peelable, it resists moisture and stains; grease-resistant but will not withstand extreme physical abuse.

Areas of use: All areas, especially kitchens and baths.

Removal hints: Peel or pull the decorative layer away from the paper backing, which will remain on the wall. Then, apply a wallcovering remover. Use a wall scraper to scrape away the backing paper.

TYPE: In-register paper-backed vinyl

Characteristics: Solid vinyl layer of material is laminated or bonded to a paper backing sheet. These wallcoverings have a heat-embossed (raised) effect to register (fit) the pattern design, and provide a multitude of textural effects.

Benefits: High-quality appearance; very durable because the decorative surface is solid vinyl; resists moisture, stains and grease; scrubbable and peelable but will not withstand extreme physical abuse.

Areas of use: All areas.

Removal hints: Peel or pull the decorative surface away from the paper backing, which will remain on the wall. Apply wallcovering remover; use a scraper to scrape away backing.

TYPE: Fabric-backed vinyl (non woven)

Characteristics: A completely synthetic product; non-woven backing is laminated to vinyl prior to printing; it is usually nonpasted.

Benefits: Manufactured in a variety of widths; resists stains and grease; durable, scrubbable and dry-strippable; high degree of mildew resistance.

Areas of use: All areas in a home or business.

Removal hints: Pull the wallcovering from the wall at a 45-degree angle. (Pulling at a 90-degree angle may damage the wall surface.)

TYPE: Fabric-backed vinyl (woven/cotton scrim)

Characteristics: Scrim backing provides structural strength; woven substrate is laminated to a decorative solid-vinyl surface.

Benefits: Durable, stain- and fade-resistant; scrubbable; dry-strippable; resists tears and creases; moisture- and grease-resistant.

Areas of use: All areas, although usually used for commercial purposes.

Removal hints: Pull the wallcovering from the wall at a 45-degree angle. (Pulling at a 90-degree angle may damage the wall surface.)

TYPE: Expanded vinyl/paintable wallcovering

Characteristics: An "expanding agent," added to liquid vinyl, makes the wallcovering expand in size after it is heated at high temperatures, producing a three-dimensional effect. Vinyl is printed on a paper substrate and may be strippable or peelable.

Benefits: Unique and dramatic appearance; retains three-dimensional effect after hanging; good for imperfect walls, over paneling or concrete blocks; usually prepasted and paintable.

Areas of use: Larger walls, where the design and visual effect can be seen to best advantage; covers defects in wall surfaces but is not suitable for areas requiring frequent cleaning.

Removal hints: Peel or pull the decorative surface away from the substrate, which will remain on the wall. Apply a wallcovering remover; use a wall scraper to scrape away substrate.

TYPE: Natural fibers

Characteristics: Natural materials, such as vines, jute, cork, hemp, cotton, silk or linen fibers that have been dyed and laminated to a paper backing. After lamination, the product is printed, using conventional methods. There will be some shading, as the wallcoverings are natural materials. They are usually unpasted.

Benefits: Provide a natural and textured character to decoration; available in an extensive variety of color combinations.

Negatives: Cannot withstand moisture; not washable or color-fast; will show fading, if exposed to sunlight (pictures, furniture and wall hangings will leave a mark if the wall is exposed to light).

Areas of use: Ideal for low-traffic areas, such as living and dining rooms.

Removal hints: Wet the surface with wallcovering remover. When saturated, peel away from the paper substrate. Saturate the substrate with remover solution and let soak for 10 to 20 minutes. Use a wall scraper to remove the substrate.

TYPE: Bridging material (Cover Ups™)

Characteristics: A porous under-wallcovering material designed to cover irregularities on walls and provide a smooth surface on which to hang decorative wallcovering.

Benefits: Covers cracks, rough plaster, paneling, concrete blocks and lightly stuccoed walls.

Areas of use: Wherever the surface is irregular, such as rough plaster, concrete blocks, stucco and metal.

Removal hints: Remove top layer of wallcovering. Soak with wallcovering remover and scrape away any remaining paper backing.

Distance around room	Ceiling height in feet. Number of double roll bolts needed			Distance around room
	8'	9'	10'	
10	2	2	3	3.0
20	4	4	5	6.0
36	7	8	9	10.9
40	8	9	9	12.1
44	8	9	10	13.3
48	9	10	11	14.5
52	10	11	12	15.8
56	11	12	13	17.0
60	11	13	14	18.2
64	12	13	15	19.4
68	13	14	16	20.6
72	13	15	17	21.8
76	14	16	18	23.0
In feet	2.4 m	2.7 m	3.0 m	In meters
	Ceiling height in meters			

How to calculate the quantity of wallcovering you'll need.

SELECTING THE "RIGHT" WALLCOVERING

Consider the following when selecting wallcovering:

- the overall color scheme you have selected
- the "look" and effect you want to achieve (is your decor style traditional, elegant, upscale, casual, country or contemporary?)
- the use for which it is intended (kitchens and busy hallways, for example, need sturdy wallcoverings)
- the condition of the walls (are the walls already textured? Is there a lot of moisture?)
- price (how much do you want to spend?)

WALLCOVERING CLEANUPS

Follow these steps when cleaning washable wallcoverings:

- start from the bottom of the wall and work up
- gently sponge with low-sudsing detergent in warm water
- rinse thoroughly with clean warm water, using a sponge
- do not use abrasive cleansers
- dry with a soft lint-free cloth

Specific instructions, including washability, scrubbability, stain-resistance and abrasion-resistance are included on every roll of wallcovering. Follow individual manufacturer's instructions.

Be sure to take action if you notice any discoloration on wallcoverings: it may be due to the presence of mildew, a pesky fungal growth that flourishes in moist dark environments, such as basements, bathrooms and closets. Wash the affected walls with a mixture of equal parts household bleach and water. Scrub with a medium-soft brush, keeping the surface wet until the discoloration is eliminated. Rinse thoroughly with warm clear water and allow to dry. To prevent mildew from forming under newly hung wallcoverings, be sure to use the paste or adhesive recommended by the manufacturer.

CALCULATING QUANTITIES

Follow these easy directions, then take your measurements to the store where you are planning to buy your paper. The staff will help you figure out your exact requirements or confirm that you have calculated correctly.

The quick method for assessing approximate amounts

Estimate the number of rolls you need to buy by measuring the distance around the perimeter of your room. (If there are window or door openings, simply measure right over them.) Measure the height of the room. Use the chart below to determine the approximate number of double rolls you require. A double roll covers approximately 44 square feet after matching patterns.

Then, count the number of openings (doors, windows, built-in cabinets or bookshelves, fireplaces, etc.) that will not be covered. Deduct one double roll for every three openings from the chart's suggested requirements. (See previous page.) This should provide an accurate estimate of the number of double rolls needed.

An alternative quick way to estimate the number of double rolls you require is simply to multiply the height measurement by the perimeter measurement and divide by 44. Then, deduct one double roll for every three openings.

How to estimate the number of rolls needed for a room with a cathedral ceiling

1. MEASURE THE ROOM
- Draw a room diagram, showing doors, windows and both minimum and maximum ceiling heights.
- Using a steel tape measure, measure and mark on the diagram:
  - wall height from floor to ceiling, excluding baseboard and moldings, at the lowest and highest points of the ceiling
  - width of each wall, including doors and windows
  - measure doors, windows and architectural details, as for a standard room
- adjust for standard doors and large windows:
  - subtract 20 square feet for each standard door
  - subtract a window square footage only if it is more than 15 square feet
- adjust for other architectural details, such as fireplaces, built-in bookcases and nonstandard doors and windows
  - calculate the area that will not require wallcovering
  - subtract this from the total wall surface

2. CALCULATE THE AREAS TO BE COVERED
- Calculate each wall separately as some may be standard height walls and some may have a cathedral ceiling. Add up the square footage of each wall. (Do not adjust for doors or windows yet.)
- To calculate the square footage of a cathedral

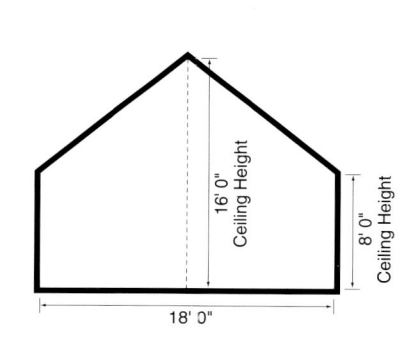

Cathedral Ceiling Wall

$\frac{8 \text{ ft.} + 16 \text{ ft.}}{2} = 12 \text{ ft.}$ *(average wall height)*

18 ft. x 12 ft. = 216 sq. ft.
x 2 *(for two cathedral ceiling walls)*
= 432 sq. ft.

Standard Walls

20 ft. x 8 ft. = 160 sq. ft. *(fireplace wall)*
20 ft. x 8 ft. = 160 sq. ft. *(front door wall)*

 432 sq. ft.
+ 160 sq. ft.
+ 160 sq. ft.
= 752 sq. ft.

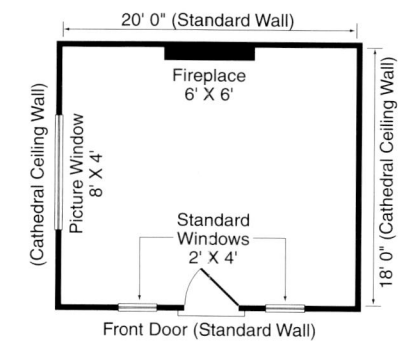

 752 sq. ft.
− 20 sq. ft. *(front door)*
− 48 sq. ft. *(windows)*
− 36 sq. ft. *(fireplace)*
= 648 sq. ft.

Usable yield = 44 sq. ft.

$\frac{648 \text{ sq. ft.}}{44 \text{ sq. ft.}} = 14.70$

= 15 DOUBLE ROLLS

ceiling wall, measure the height of the wall at the highest point and at the shortest point. Add these measurements together and divide by two. This gives you an average wall height. Multiply by the wall's width to get the square footage of this wall.

- Subtract area of doors, windows and architectural details, as for a standard room. (See above.)
- Now, you have the total square footage to be covered. Divide by 44 and round up to determine the number of rolls required.

How to estimate the number of rolls needed for a stairway with a ceiling rise

1. MEASURE ACCURATELY
- Measure as for a standard room, but also measure the rise of the stairway and the ceiling. Ceiling and stairway rises are nearly always the same. This is your vertical measurement.

2. CALCULATE THE AREA TO BE COVERED
- Divide the area into triangles ("A" and "C" in the diagram) and, if necessary, a rectangle ("B" in diagram). Calculate the rectangle by multiplying the length times the rise, and triangles as two thirds the length times the rise. Add the totals of these individual areas to determine the total wall surface to be covered.
- Now, you have the square footage to be covered. Divide by 44 and round up to determine the number of rolls required.

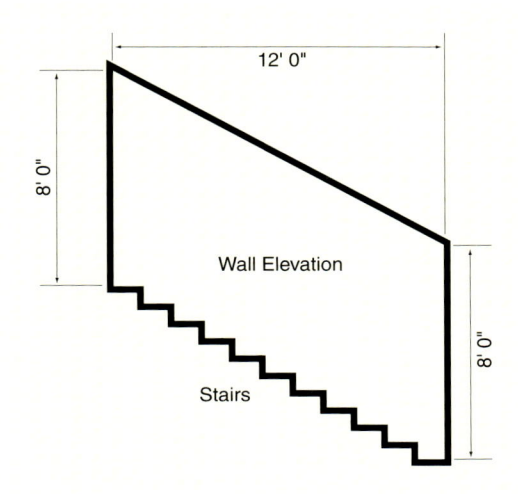

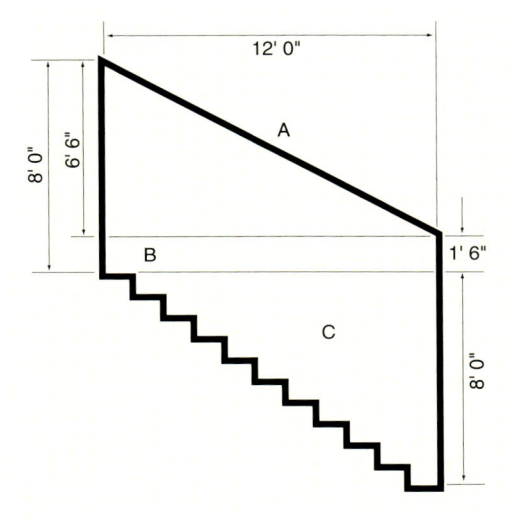

A = (12 ft. x 6.5 ft.) = 78 sq. ft. x $2/3$ = 52 sq. ft.

B = 12 ft. x 1.5 ft. = 18 sq. ft.

C = (12 ft. x 8 ft.) = 96 sq. ft. x $2/3$ = 64 sq. ft.

Total wall surface = A + B + C
= 134 sq. ft.

Usable yield = 44 sq. ft.

134 ÷ 44 = 2.3
= 3 DOUBLE ROLLS

> ### WISE ADVICE FROM THE PROS
>
> - When determining the number of rolls you require, always round up the number, if your calculations include a partial roll. This way, you will be certain to have enough of the same dye lot.
>
> - Be sure all rolls are from the same dye lot and run number — otherwise they may not match perfectly. The only time you may mix lots is when an entire wall has been completed: if necessary, you may start an adjacent wall with a roll from another dye lot and probably not see a difference. Always make a note of the dye-lot number, pattern number and collection name of the wallcovering and store it in a safe place.
>
> - Buy an extra roll of wallcovering, in case an area is damaged later. Sometimes, on a very large repeat pattern, there may be less waste per roll if you work from several rolls at once.
>
> - It is unwise to hang new wallcovering over an existing wallcovering. Several problems may occur if you do. The old paper may bubble, which cannot be smoothed out. The colors of the old paper may bleed through the new, and the old seams may show under the new paper. If there is no alternative and you must hang a new wallcovering over old paper, first sand down all existing seams. Make sure any bubbles are removed. Apply an oil-base primer over the entire area, followed by size, before hanging new wallcovering.
>
> - For difficult-to-remove wallcoverings, use a chemical stripper. First, score the old covering with a toothed wheel (available at home-decorating centers) and give the chemicals time to work before trying to remove the covering. (Do not use steamers to remove wallcoverings. They can be dangerous and may damage drywall.) Once the covering has been removed from the wall, wash with a mild detergent and water and rinse. Prepare as you would any other wall.

PATTERN-MATCH REPEATS

Wallcovering patterns are printed in repeats known as straight match, random match, drop matches and free match. When you buy wallcoverings based on 44 square feet of coverage per double roll, this figure allows for enough wallcovering for you to match patterns. For those patterns with no match, you will actually get more than 44 square feet of coverage. Generally, you get four eight-foot strips of wallcovering per double roll.

STRAIGHT MATCH A straight match is one in which the pattern match flows directly across the strips. When hung, every strip will be the same at the ceiling line, and the same part of the pattern in the first and following strips will be the same distance from the ceiling.

RANDOM MATCH A random match is one in which the pattern matches, no matter how the adjoining strips are positioned. Grasscloth and vertical stripes are common random matches.

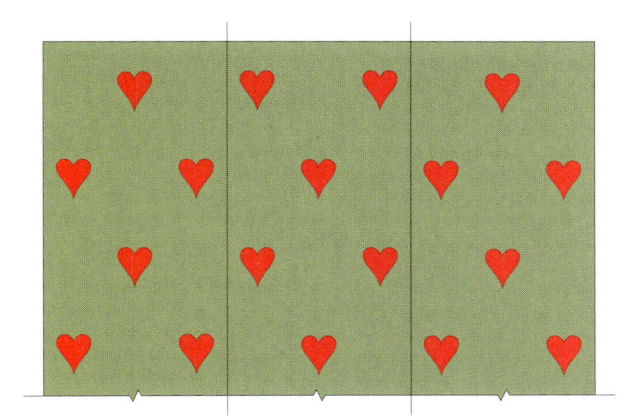

HALF-DROP MATCH A drop match design does not run in a straight line across the wall. Instead, it appears to run diagonally. In a half-drop match, the design is staggered, so that only every other strip is identical at the ceiling line. It takes two strips of wallcovering to complete the pattern horizontally.

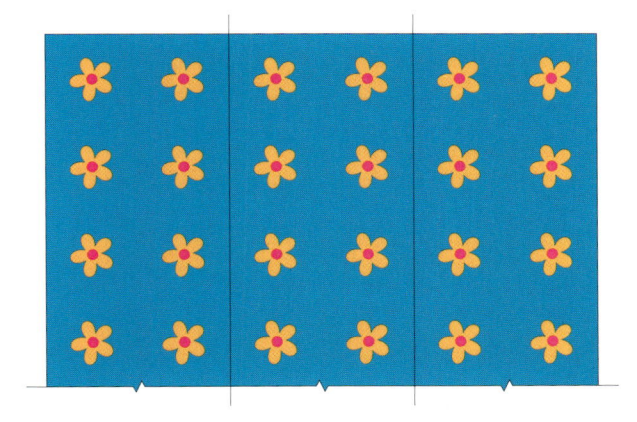

FREE MATCH Most other patterns are easy to match because the design is split at the seams. However, in some patterns, the design is not split at the seams: this is called a free match. Free-match patterns may have straight-across matches or drop matches. You will need to line up design elements, rather than match segments of a divided pattern.

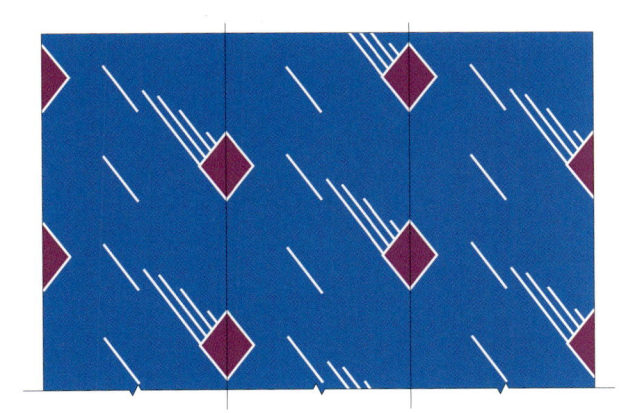

MULTIPLE-DROP MATCH In multiple-drop patterns, it can take three, four or five strips of wallcovering for the pattern to complete itself. A one-third-drop pattern requires three strips to complete the pattern and four to repeat. A one-quarter-drop pattern requires four strips to complete the pattern and five to repeat, and so on.

Wallcovering Basics 31

The best tools for the best results. Clockwise, from the top: water tray, sponge, wall size, putty knife with flexible blade, sandpaper, scissors, razor knife, pencil, trim guide, plumb line with bob and chalk, seam roller, smoothing brush, trim guide and smoother. Don't forget a drop cloth to protect your flooring, a work table to spread out the wallcovering and a stepladder to get to the top. A level, tape measure and steel straight edge are also useful tools.

CHAPTER 5

Ready, Set, Go!

PREPARE THE SURFACE

For the average do-it-yourselfer, hanging wallcoverings is quick and easy, even if you've never done it before. However, to guarantee satisfactory results, there are certain steps that must be followed, including special preparatory treatments.

First, you must prepare the walls to receive the covering. This is the foundation for a good job. Most walls need some preparation — even those in new homes. Time spent on surface prep work will make the task of hanging wallcoverings easier and will help ensure satisfactory results that will look beautiful for years to come. **Check the instructions included with your wallcovering for the manufacturer's recommendations.** Before beginning any surface preparation, remove all nails, screws, electrical plates and any other wall fixtures. Remove all old wallcovering. (Refer to pages 25 to 27 for instructions on the removal of various types of wallcoverings.) Make sure the surface is free of mildew, grease or other stains. Scrape off any loose paint.

Note these general instructions, then consult the chart on page 34 for directions on preparing special surfaces.

For **new undecorated walls and new drywall**, make sure the surface is dry and clean before you begin. Apply a high-quality primer/sealer (see page 34), which will give the wallcovering an even surface to adhere to. Use a white-pigmented sealer, because colored primers may bleed through the wallcovering. Follow the manufacturer's directions for drying and curing, then apply a cold-water size (see page 34) to make it easier to hang and position wallcovering and to remove it later. Let dry for about 30 minutes before hanging wallcovering.

For **previously papered walls**, remove all the old wallcovering, then clean the bare walls with a mild detergent solution (*not T.S.P. — tri-sodium phosphate*) or adhesive remover. Rinse with clear water and allow to dry thoroughly. Then, apply a cold-water size (see page 34). It is always best to remove old coverings. If this is not possible, ensure that the old covering is secure and stable, sand the seams, then prime with an oil-base primer and size before applying a new wallcovering.

For **previously painted walls**, scrape or sand off any rough spots and fill holes and cracks with spackling compound (see page 34). Let dry, then sand smooth. Apply an oil-base primer to spackled areas. Let dry. For surfaces painted with glossy paint, sand all over with fine-grit sandpaper. Rinse wall with clear water and allow to dry thoroughly. Apply a cold-water size to improve positioning and adhesion. Let dry before hanging wallcovering.

SURFACE	PREPARATION	PRIMER	SPECIAL NEEDS
Flat paint, water-sensitive	If peeling or unstable, scrape, sand, rinse	High-quality primer; size	Wash as needed
Flat paint, good-quality	Clean with clear water	High-quality primer; size	
Sand-finish, paint, stucco	Scrape, sand smooth	High-quality primer; size; apply Cover-Ups™; size	Lining paper (Cover Ups™); requires pasting
Gloss paint	Wash, dry, sand (120-grit); rinse	High-quality primer; size	
Textured paint	Scrape, sand smooth; rinse over Cover Ups™	High quality primer; size	Lining paper (Cover Ups™)
Calcimine (white wash)	Wash from surface	High-quality primer; size	Wash as needed
New plaster	Cure for 30 - 60 days; sand smooth	High-quality primer; size	
New drywall	Sand seams smooth, if necessary	High-quality primer; size	Level up recessed nails with Spackle
Cinder block	Flush joints; drywall compound to make surface smooth	High-quality primer; apply Cover Ups™; size	Skim-coat seam areas; block-filler; treat for excess acidity/alkalinity, as necessary
Wood paneling	Sand, rinse, fill grooves	High-quality primer; apply Cover Ups™; size	Lining paper (Cover Ups™)
New plywood or particle-board	Sand smooth; Spackle joints	High-quality primer; size	Fiberglass joint tape
New Masonite	Sand smooth; Spackle joints	High-quality primer; size	Fiberglass joint tape
Metal surface	Wash; file rough edges	Metal primer; then high-quality primer; size	Nonrusting metal primer

Preparing walls for wallcoverings is easy if you follow these instructions.

Wall Preparation

All surfaces must be clean, smooth, stable and free of nails, screws, etc., before the wallcovering is applied.

GET THE HANG OF HANGING WALLCOVERINGS

Before you begin, read the directions on the wallcovering.

1. Get it straight!

Start with a straight line. To make sure your first strip and those that follow it are perfectly straight, use a chalked plumb line (see page 32). Here's how:

- Choose an inconspicuous corner, preferably one behind a door. (This is where you'll begin hanging the covering.) Measure out from the corner on the wall to the right to a point that is one-half inch narrower than the width of the wallcovering. Make a mark on the wall at this point at ceiling height to show where you'll draw your plumb line, using a plumb bob or a weighted string rubbed with soft or powdered chalk.
- Tack the end of the line or string at your mark at the top of the wall, so that the plumb bob's point is slightly above the baseboard.
- Press the weighted end of the string against the wall and snap the line. The resulting chalk mark is your starting line for hanging the right edge of your first strip of wallcovering.
- As an alternative, you may establish your vertical line by using a long level.

2. How high is the room?

Walls are seldom the exact same height all around, so you must measure the distance from the ceiling to the baseboard in several locations around the room in order to find the maximum height. Then, add four inches to this measurement. (This will allow for an uneven ceiling or baseboard.) This is the length you'll need to cut your first wallcovering strip.

3. Cut it out!

Patterns are designed with basic matches (see page 31). Be sure to check the proper pattern match before you cut.

- Using the maximum wall height and the extra four inches you added, cut your first strip.
- Next, match up the second strip with the pattern of the first strip, making sure you have enough wallcovering to match the first strip at both the top and bottom.
- Hang the first strip (see next step), then cut the third strip to match up to the second.
- Continue like this, cutting only one strip at a time, making sure the patterns match and that there is enough wallcovering at both the top and bottom. If you are using a wallcovering with a large pattern repeat, work from more than one roll at a time; you may find that there is less waste.

Use a chalked plumb line to make sure your strips are straight.

Dip the strip in water for the recommended length of time.

4. Prepare the prepasted wallcovering

Since most wallcoverings are prepasted, your next steps are as follows:

- Place a water tray half full of water (at the temperature specified in the directions) at the foot of a work surface or table.
- Loosely roll up the cut-to-size strip with the pattern-side in.
- Dip the strip in the water and leave for the length of time recommended in the instructions found on the back of the product label (times vary). Do not leave the wallcovering in the water longer than recommended or the paste may wash away.
- When pulling the strip from the water, check for any dry spots and wet them immediately.
- Lift the strip out of the water and lay it out paste-side up on the table or other flat work surface.
- "Book" the strip by folding the pasted side of the strip to the pasted side, taking care not to crease the strip; leave for a maximum of three minutes. (Booking ensures that the paste has been given time to activate and allows the wet strip to expand before being applied to the wall. If the strip is not given time to expand, it may do so on the wall, resulting in overlapping seams.)

Line up the first strip against the plumb line.

5. Hang it!

Now you're ready!

- Line up the right edge of the first strip against the plumb line. (The left edge will tuck into the corner and attach to the adjacent wall.)
- Use a smoothing brush to press the wallcovering to the wall; move any air pockets to the edge and out. The strip should overlap the ceiling and the baseboard.

Book the strip by folding the pasted side of the strip to the pasted side.

Do not overlap strips; just butt the edges, carefully matching the pattern.

Use a razor knife and trim guide to trim any excess wallcovering.

- Hang the second strip. Do not overlap the strips; just butt the edges. Do not push or pull the seams into place, as this may stretch the wallcovering. Move the entire strip by lifting and sliding it over, if necessary.
- Make sure the strips are tight against each other and against the wall. Always match the pattern at eye level first and then work up to the top and down to the bottom.
- Using a razor knife and trim guide, carefully trim off any excess wallcovering at the top and bottom.
- Make sure the seam is tight together. Use a seam roller to roll the seam lightly.
- Sponge off any extra paste with clean water and dry off with a soft cloth.
- **After you have hung two strips, inspect carefully for problems in color shading, pattern matches or other defects. If there is a problem, return the wallcovering to the store.**
- Proceeding to the right, continue around the room until the wall is completely covered.
- When you reach a corner, cut the strip of wallpaper to the required width to finish that wall plus an extra half inch, to allow for corner overlap, before wetting.
- After applying this strip, draw a plumb line on the next wall (at the width of the leftover strip) and apply the balance of the cut strip, fitting it into the corner to overlap the previous strip slightly. This ensures that the wallcovering is hung plumb on every wall.
- Applying vinyl-to-vinyl adhesive at corners is sometimes recommended to prevent edges from coming loose.

Wallcovering a ceiling

To attach wallcovering to a ceiling, prepare the surface in the same way you would prepare wall surfaces.

- Gather together all the proper tools, including ladders or a scaffold, smoother, seam roller, sponge, cutter, straight edge, commercial wallcovering paste, brush and someone to help you — wallcovering a ceiling is much easier when you work with someone else. You'll need a solid platform on which to stand. Sawhorses spanned with boards work well, because you can travel some distance along them and your head will be about a foot from the ceiling, which is ideal.
- If you are using the same covering as on the wall, determine where to hang the first strip by matching it to the seam of a strip already hung on the wall. If the wall strip's seam is six inches out from the corner, mark the ceiling at this

You'll need someone to help you wallpaper a ceiling.

point all the way across: this will give you a straight line.

- Cut the first strip about three inches longer than the width of the ceiling. (If the wallcovering is prepasted, don't wet it.) Lay the strips out on the work table. Then, use a wallpaper brush to apply commercial wallcovering paste, which will guarantee a good solid bond.
- "Book" the strip by folding it paste-side to paste-side and let it sit for three minutes (or according to the instructions on the adhesive), so that the paste sinks into the paper.
- Apply the strip to the ceiling along the marked line. Start in the center and work to either end. Smooth the strip out from the center, removing air bubbles.
- Apply the second strip, matching patterns. Trim the edges.
- Roll the seam and rinse both strips with a damp sponge.
- Continue across the ceiling.

Decorating with Wallcovering Borders

Wallcovering borders are available in myriad styles, including intricate precision die-cut patterns and pierced patterns. They add style, define a space, highlight architectural features and create new lines. Often placed at the ceiling, they may also be used around doors and windows and as a chair rail or wainscotting detail one-third the way up a wall or to create wall panels. Borders at the top of walls draw the eye upwards. Hung at picture-rail height a foot or so below the ceiling, the effect is to lower the ceiling.

- If the walls are freshly covered with a wallcovering, they should be left to dry for the length of time recommended by the manufacturer before applying a border. If the walls are freshly painted with latex paint, allow the paint to cure for 30 days before a border is applied. Then, apply size to the area over which the border will be hung. (Note: Mark a line about one-quarter inch narrower than the width of the border and size only within this area, to avoid having to touch up areas above and/or below the border.)

Cut the border strip long enough to allow for overlapping and mitering.

Use a razor knife and straight edge to cut through both layers at a 45-degree angle. Peel back and remove the excess borders.

- Measuring the amount of border to buy is easy, and since it is done in linear footage (not square footage), calculations are quick to make. If you are applying a border at ceiling height or as a chair rail, simply measure the entire distance around the perimeter of the room. Allow a little extra to compensate for walls that are out of plumb and for matching patterns when joining rolls.

- Applying a border is simple. If the surface you are covering is slick or shiny, it's important to size the area, as described above. If the border is being applied over a vinyl wallcovering, use vinyl-to-vinyl adhesive or special border adhesive recommended by the manufacturer.
- If you are applying a prepasted border, loosely roll the pattern inside and immerse in water. Read the instructions on the roll for the water temperature and length of soaking time. Slowly draw out the roll, making sure that the back (paste) is completely wet. Do not leave the border in the water longer than the recommended time or all the paste may wash away.
- Place the border on a flat work surface. "Book" the border by folding paste-side to paste-side and pattern to pattern in an accordion fashion. Leave for no more than three minutes before hanging. This allows the border time to absorb water and the paper fibers to relax.
- Start hanging a border in an inconspicuous corner, overlapping it one-half inch over the corner onto the adjacent wall. Gradually unfold as you smooth the border into position on the wall; rinse thoroughly as you proceed.
- At inside corners, cut the border to tuck in about 1/4 inch onto next wall and trim. Start the next wall by hanging the rest of the border, overlapping the 1/4 inch in the corner.
- When you come to the end of a strip, match the pattern with the next border strip. Overlap the two borders at the match. Using a razor knife, cut through the two borders on a diagonal. Peel back both edges and remove the overlap. Smooth back into place and wipe away excess paste.
- If you are planning to hang borders around windows or doorways, measure the amount required. Take into account that, at the corners, you will need to add to your measurements the depth of each border strip to allow for overlapping or mitering. (Use a border pattern that does not have a strong directional print to avoid pattern mismatches at each corner.)
- For a miter cut, simply overlap the two border ends where they meet at the corners. Using a razor knife and straight edge, carefully cut through both layers at a 45-degree angle.
- Gently peel back and remove the excess borders. Press the joint flat.
- Use a damp sponge to remove any adhesive from the seam.
- If you are using a border as a chair rail over a painted wall, prep the wall, as described above. Then, use a level to draw two parallel lines the width of the border and use these as a guide for placing the border on the wall.

WISE ADVICE FROM THE PROS

- When applying wallcovering over new drywall, be sure to seal the surface properly with a high-quality primer, followed by size. It is almost impossible to remove wallcoverings from unsealed drywall without seriously damaging the surface of the wall.

- Turn off the electrical power when trimming around outlets and switches.

- Don't attempt your first wallcovering project in the kitchen or bathroom. Although often small, these rooms have many complicated spots to cover.

- If you are planning to paint the ceiling, moldings, trim or doors in a room, do so before you hang the wallcovering.

- Prick air pockets with a pin to release trapped air. Dampen area with a wet sponge and resmooth.

Durable vinyl-coated wallcoverings brighten the walls and ceiling; coordinated fabrics decorate the windows and cushions.

CHAPTER 6

The Well-Dressed Home

WELCOME HOME!

Imagine this exciting scenario: you and your furnishings have arrived at your new home. Even if someone else has lived there before, this home is new to you. You may find room after room awaiting your personal decorating touch to turn the place from a stranger's house into *your* home. Or you may have a blank canvas of fresh drywall to decorate with your own palette of colors and patterns. Either way, the fun is about to begin.

Over the next few pages, you'll see how glorious wallcoverings can change a basic builder's house from boring to beautiful. Pick the ideas that suit your tastes, the look you love or the ambience you want to create in your home.

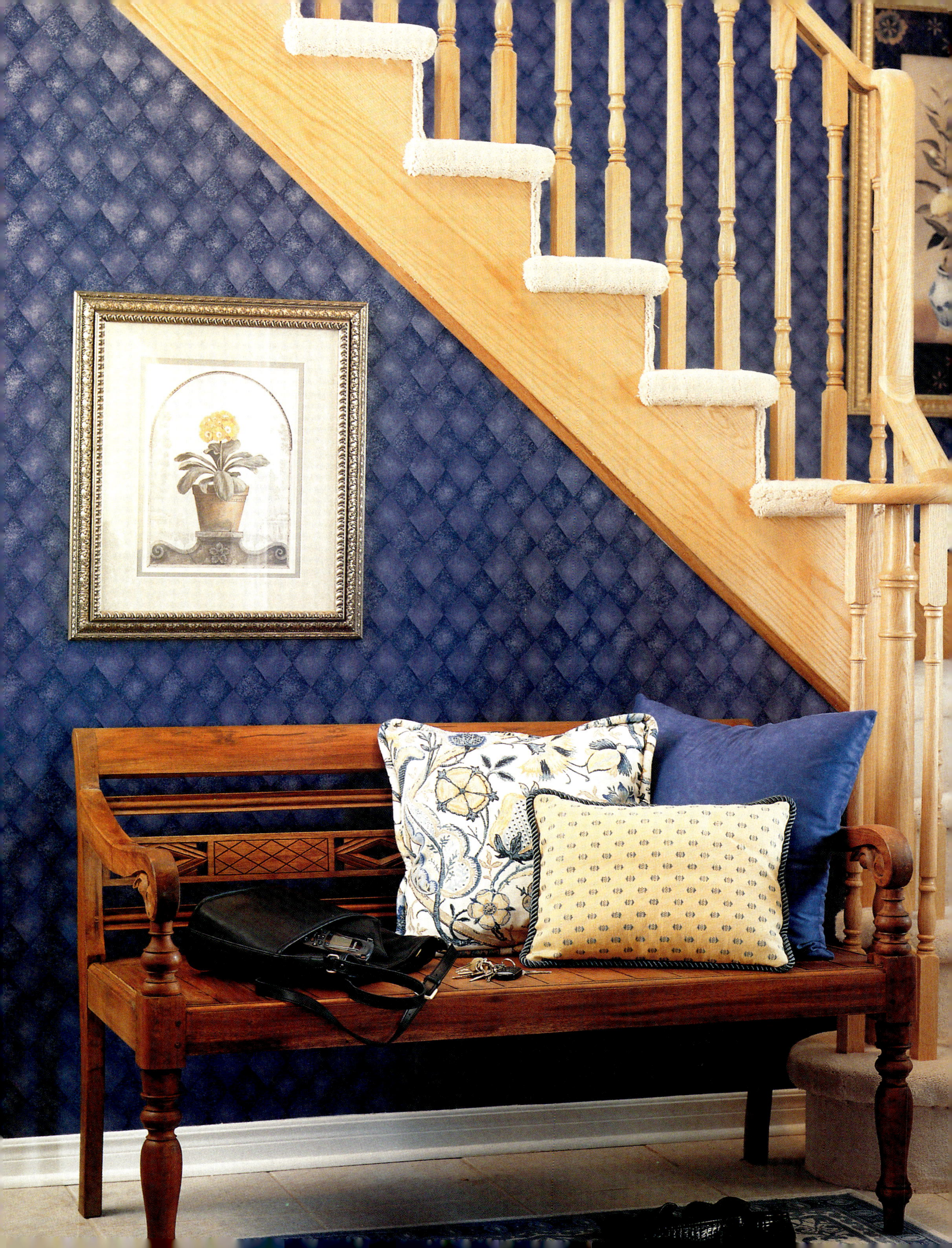

Inviting Entrance Hall

Every entrance says "welcome" in its own special way. The entry that is large enough for a chair or bench on which to sit to remove boots or to drop parcels and papers is particularly welcoming.

Here, a deep-blue wallcovering, subtly patterned with tone-on-tone harlequin-shaped diamonds, creates an immediate sense of intimacy. The impact of this is particularly dramatic when contrasted with the open bright airiness of the other main-floor rooms, all of which are visible from the entrance.

Various shades of blue appear elsewhere: in the living room, on the kitchen ceiling, in the dining-room and kitchen wallcoverings and in furniture and accessories throughout. The entire main floor is tied together by the reappearance of similar colors. But nowhere is the blue as bold as it is in this welcoming entrance.

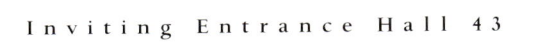

BEFORE

Wallcovering is a solid vinyl. McCall's Home Decorating patterns for the cushions #8081 and #9260.

The Well-Dressed Home 44

Sunny Family/Living Room

(Photo page 40)
McCall's Home Dec-in-a-Sec™ pattern for the window treatment #8772; McCall's Home Decorating patterns for the cushions #8081 and #9260.

Perfect for family living or for special entertaining, this bright and cheerful living room makes every day seem warm and sunny. A subtle ragged texture adds dimension to the tone-on-tone striped wallcovering; coordinating fabrics highlight the windows in style. A pastel faux-marble covering on the soaring cathedral ceiling stretches into the kitchen — the perfect solution to a challenging transition between these two open-concept rooms. The same faux-marble covering decorates the columns dividing the living and dining rooms, further unifying the three primary main-floor rooms.

With faux-finish wallcoverings, you are always guaranteed uniform pattern everywhere, unlike paint, where the application may be lighter or heavier in different areas.

Comfortable and child-friendly, the sofas sport washable slipcovers. Dark wood furniture contrasts with the light-colored walls and carpet. Framed prints are hung low, so that they relate to the furniture below. Several shades of blue and yellow appear in the cozy cushions.

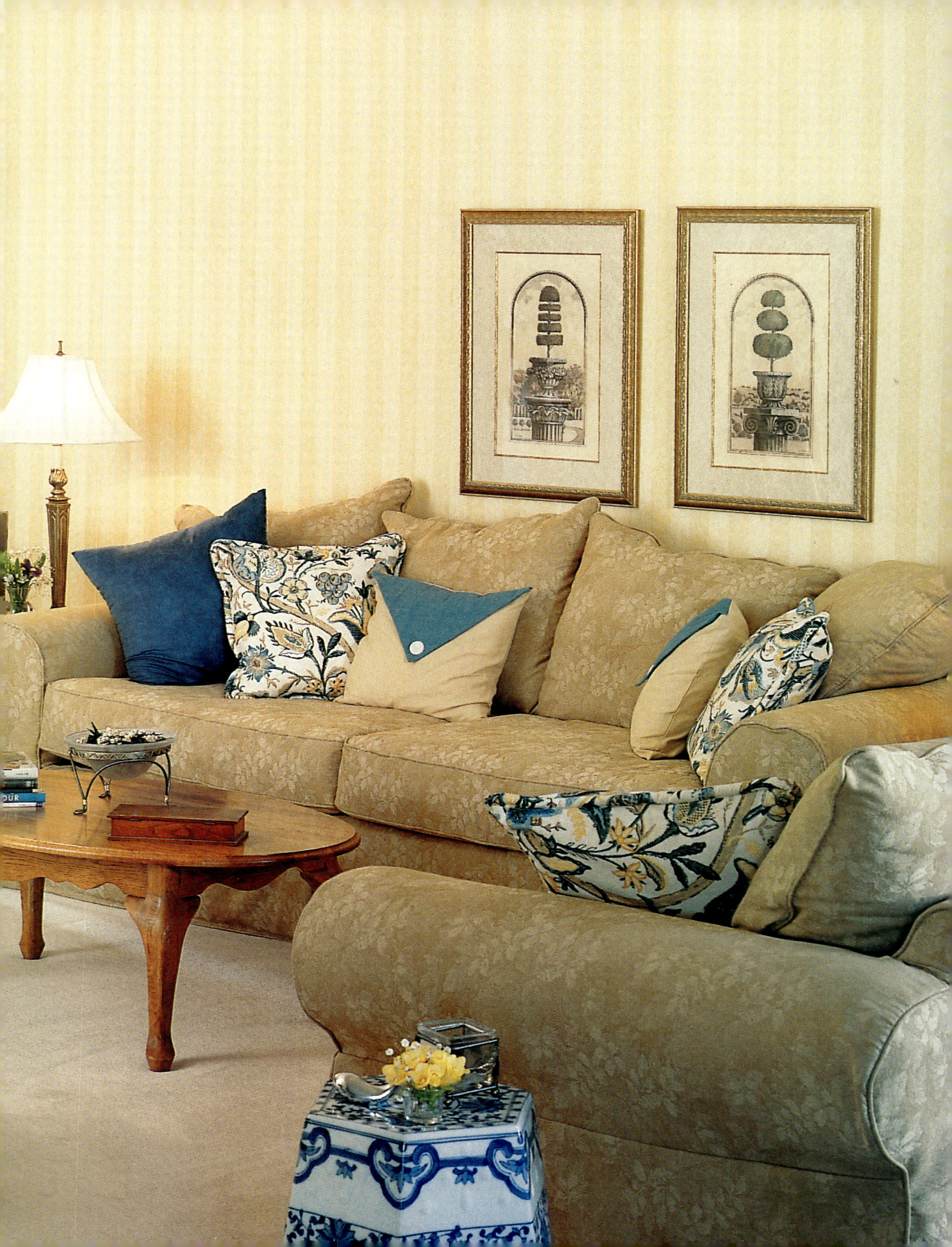

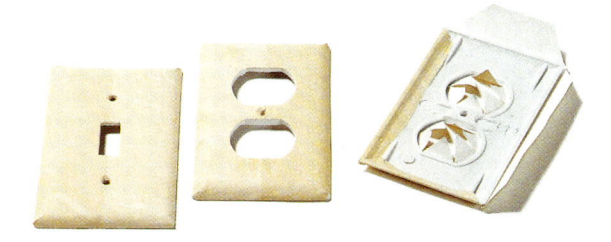

SWITCHED-ON COVERS

For a designer look, finish electrical plates and vents with wallcovering.

SUPPLIES:
- *wallcovering scraps*
- *pencil*
- *razor knife*
- *nail*
- *vinyl-to-vinyl adhesive*

METHOD:
1. Take a dry scrap piece of wallcovering that roughly matches the area where the plate is located and hold it against the wall over the outlet or switchplate. Mark the corners of the plate with a sharp pencil point. Remove the plate.
2. Cut out a piece of wallcovering about one inch larger than the size of the plate marked by the four corners. Mark on the underside of the wallcovering where the switch or outlet holes occur.
3. Use a razor knife to cut two lines in each hole, corner to corner on the diagonal, thus producing four triangular-shaped flaps in each hole.
4. Paste the front of the plate and the back of the wallcovering with vinyl-to-vinyl adhesive. (Note that some chrome and plastic plates may require a primer coat so that the adhesive will hold.)
5. Lay the wallcovering over the front of the plate, taking care that the corners are properly located. Cut across the corners on the diagonal.
6. Wrap the excess wallcovering around the plate, tucking in the edges and pressing firmly until the adhesive is set. Press the flaps in the holes to the underside and hold until set.
7. After the adhesive is thoroughly dry, use a nail to poke a hole through the screw openings. Remount the plates for a perfect match!

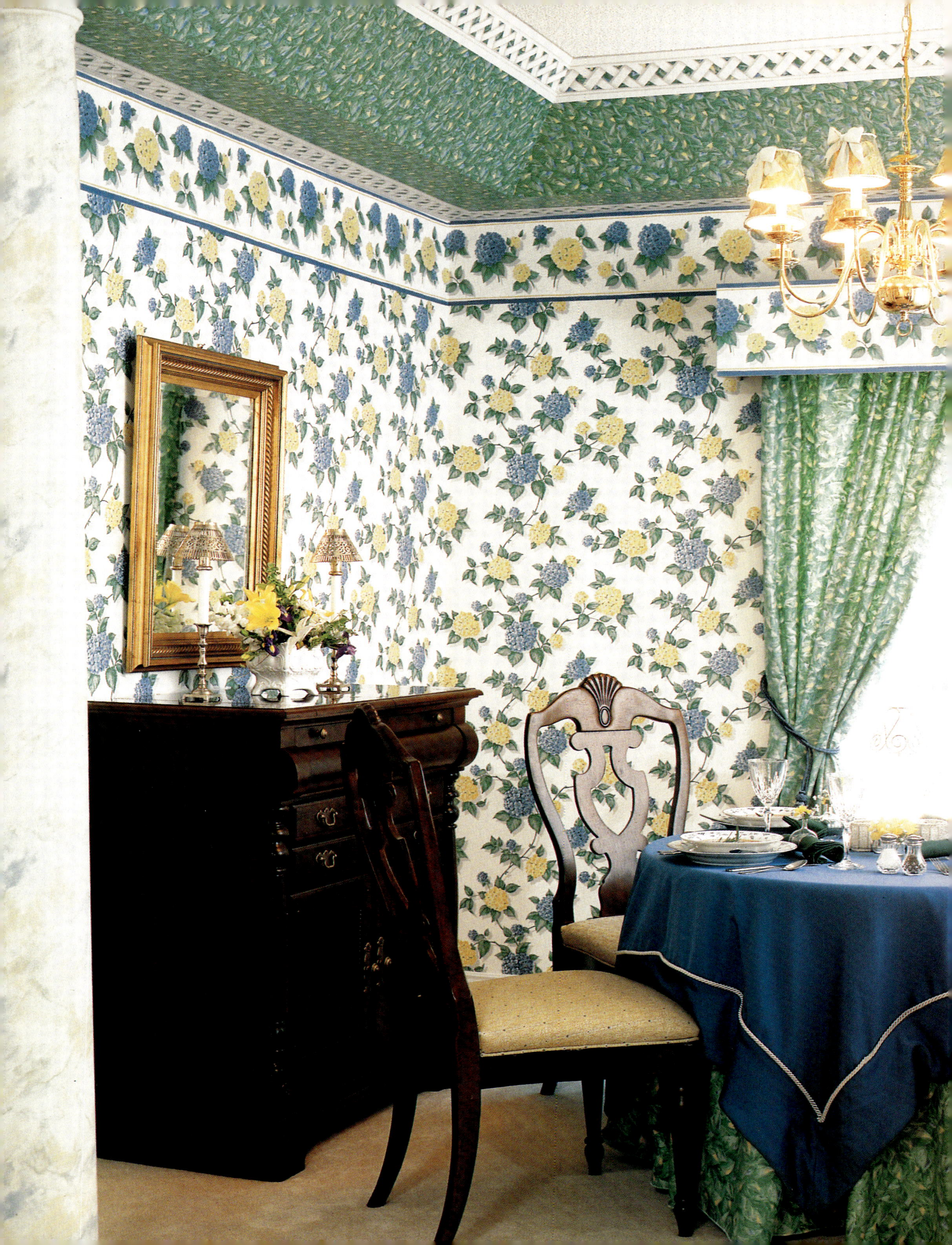

Distinctively Dramatic Dining Room

The creative use of coordinating patterns and assertive colors makes the dining room, with its unique coffered ceiling, one of the most vibrant areas of the house. The leafy-patterned wallcovering on the slope of the ceiling (repeated in the fabric used for the drapes and the table-skirt) and lattice die-cut border tie the room together and create a summer gazebo effect. A window valance and chandelier shades covered with wallcoverings prove that small decorative accents can make a big impact. The refreshing hydrangea wallcovering and 10-inch border boldly repeat the colors in the living room and kitchen; the columns take their cue from the ceiling in these adjacent rooms.

BEFORE

PRETTY-UP PILLARS

Use a faux wallcovering to dress up columns.

SUPPLIES:
- *oil-base primer*
- *size*
- *wallcovering*

METHOD:
1. Pillars must be clean, smooth and dust-free. Apply an oil-base primer, let dry, then apply size. Let dry.
2. Cut a strip of wallcovering. It should be as long as the height of the pillar plus 2 inches. If the pillar is embellished with a raised pattern, it may be necessary to apply a standard wallcovering paste to the wallcovering before attaching it. Otherwise, wet the wallcovering in a water trough.
3. Wrap the strip around the pillar, positioning the vertical seam in an inconspicuous place.
4. Beginning at eye level, smooth the wallcovering against the pillar, then work towards both the top and bottom of the pillar.
5. If the pillar is tapered at the top, cut vertical slits in the wallcovering to ease in the fullness by overlapping the covering. If the pillar enlarges towards the bottom, fill in the bare area using a piece of wallcovering under the main wallcovering at the seam.
6. Smooth the wallcovering firmly in place. Wipe off excess adhesive.

WISE ADVICE FROM THE PROS
- Use a toothpick to mark nail and screw holes that you'll be wanting to use after the wallcovering project is completed. Stick the toothpick in the hole, remove it when covering over it, then push it back into the hole once the strip is affixed to the wall.

WINDOW DRESSING

Finish off a window in style with a wallcovering valance.

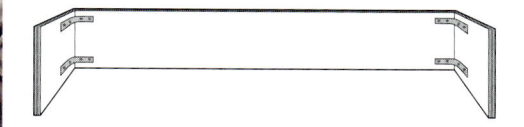

SUPPLIES:
- *wallcovering border*
- *quarter-inch-thick plywood*
- *six L-brackets*
- *screws*
- *oil-base primer*
- *size*
- *one-inch paint brush*
- *scroll saw (optional)*

METHOD:
1. Measure the width of the window outside the frame. If the valance is to cover an existing curtain rod, measure its length. Add two inches to either measurement: this will be the length of the valance. To determine the depth of the valance, measure the width of the wallcovering border. If the border is die-cut, measure to the deepest point of the pattern. If using a wallcovering, determine how much of it you want to see and cut it to this width.
2. Out of the plywood, cut the front valance panel the required length. The depth should be the same as the depth of the border. Cut two end pieces, each four inches long and the same depth as the front panel.
3. Using two L-brackets on the underside at each end, screw the end pieces to the front panel through the face of the

board. Screw the other end of the L-bracket into the side pieces.

4. Prime the wood inside and out, using an oil-base primer. Let dry, then apply size to the facing front and side panels.

5. If the border is die-cut and you want to imitate its dimensional feeling, tape a piece of border to the front and side panels and trace around it with a pencil. Use a scroll saw to cut out the design from the wood.

6. Apply the border to the valance, following the instructions on the package. Wipe off excess adhesive and allow to dry for 24 hours.

7. Use L-brackets to mount the valance to the wall.

> **WISE ADVICE FROM THE PROS**
>
> - The busier the pattern or texture, the less the seams will show.
>
> - When hanging a textured nonpatterned wallcovering, be sure to reverse the direction of each strip to help eliminate differences in shading.

Coordinated durable vinyl-coated wallcoverings brighten the dining room. Coordinating fabric dresses the window and table. McCall's Home Dec-in-a-Sec™ pattern for the draperies #8772; McCall's Home Decorating pattern for the table covering #9160.

LIGHT UP A LAMP SHADE

Match your lamp shades to your wallcovering.

SUPPLIES:
- *wire lamp shade form or lamp shade covered with stiff paper*
- *kraft paper or newspaper*
- *masking tape*
- *scissors*
- *"tacky" craft glue or hot-glue gun and glue sticks*
- *wallcovering*
- *decorative trim (available at sewing stores)*
- *ribbon*

METHOD:
1. If using a shade with existing paper covering, dust well.

2. Wrap kraft paper or newspaper around the form or shade to create a template to use as a pattern for cutting out wallcovering. Temporarily hold it in place with masking tape. Cut away the paper at the top and bottom, so that it is flush with the wire rims. Use a pencil to mark a seam line where the pieces will meet vertically. Allowing a half-inch overlap, cut away the excess.

3. Lay the template on the underside of a piece of wallcovering. Trace around the shape and cut it out.

4. Use tacky glue or a hot glue gun to attach the paper to the wire form or to the top and bottom edges of the existing shade. Glue the vertical seam and press the edges together until the glue has set. Trim the edges again, if necessary.

5. Glue decorative trim around the top and bottom edges, joining the ends at the vertical seam line. Wrap a piece of ribbon around the shade at the seam line. Attach with a dab of glue. Tie a small bow and glue to the upper rim at the ribbon line.

Pansy-printed solid vinyl wallcovering brightens the kitchen and eating nook.

Sunny Eating Nook

In the kitchen and eating nook, pretty patterned wallcoverings, stunning window treatments and country-look furniture draw the eye away from the standard cabinets, fixtures and flooring usually present in a basic builder's house. Perky pansies dot the wallcovering and border — even the backsplash. Paintable wallcovering (great for covering up cracks or flaws in the drywall) gives texture to the ceiling above the garden doors. The same stripe and fauxmarble wallcoverings of the adjoining living room unify the spaces. Coordinating plaid fabric on the windows, door and chairs provides a pattern variation, using the same colors.

McCall's Home Decorating pattern for the chair covers #8944; McCall's Home Dec-in-a-Sec™ pattern for the window treatment #8211.

Sunny Eating Nook 53

TRICKS WITH TILES

Cheer up plain ceramic tiles with wallcovering motifs.

SUPPLIES:
- *ceramic tiles*
- *motifs cut from wallcoverings*
- *vinyl-to-vinyl wallcovering adhesive*
- *sponge*
- *urethane (glossy or matt finish to match surface of tiles)*

METHOD:
1. Clean tiles thoroughly and wipe dry.
2. Apply a small amount of adhesive to the underside of the motifs, spreading it evenly and thoroughly. Press to the tile where desired.
3. Using a barely damp sponge, smooth out the motifs, wiping off any adhesive that may seep out around the edges. Let dry. Then, apply three coats of urethane, allowing to dry well between coats.

WISE ADVICE FROM THE PROS

- Do not use a seam roller when hanging flocked wallcoverings or those with raised patterns. Firmly press seams and edges with a damp sponge.

- Wash excess paste from painted and wallcovered areas before it dries.

- Do not use newspapers to cover a work table, because ink may transfer to the wallcovering.

- Change or break off a razor knife blade frequently. This will eliminate rough cuts on the wallcovering and leave a perfect trim line every time.

Sunny Eating Nook 55

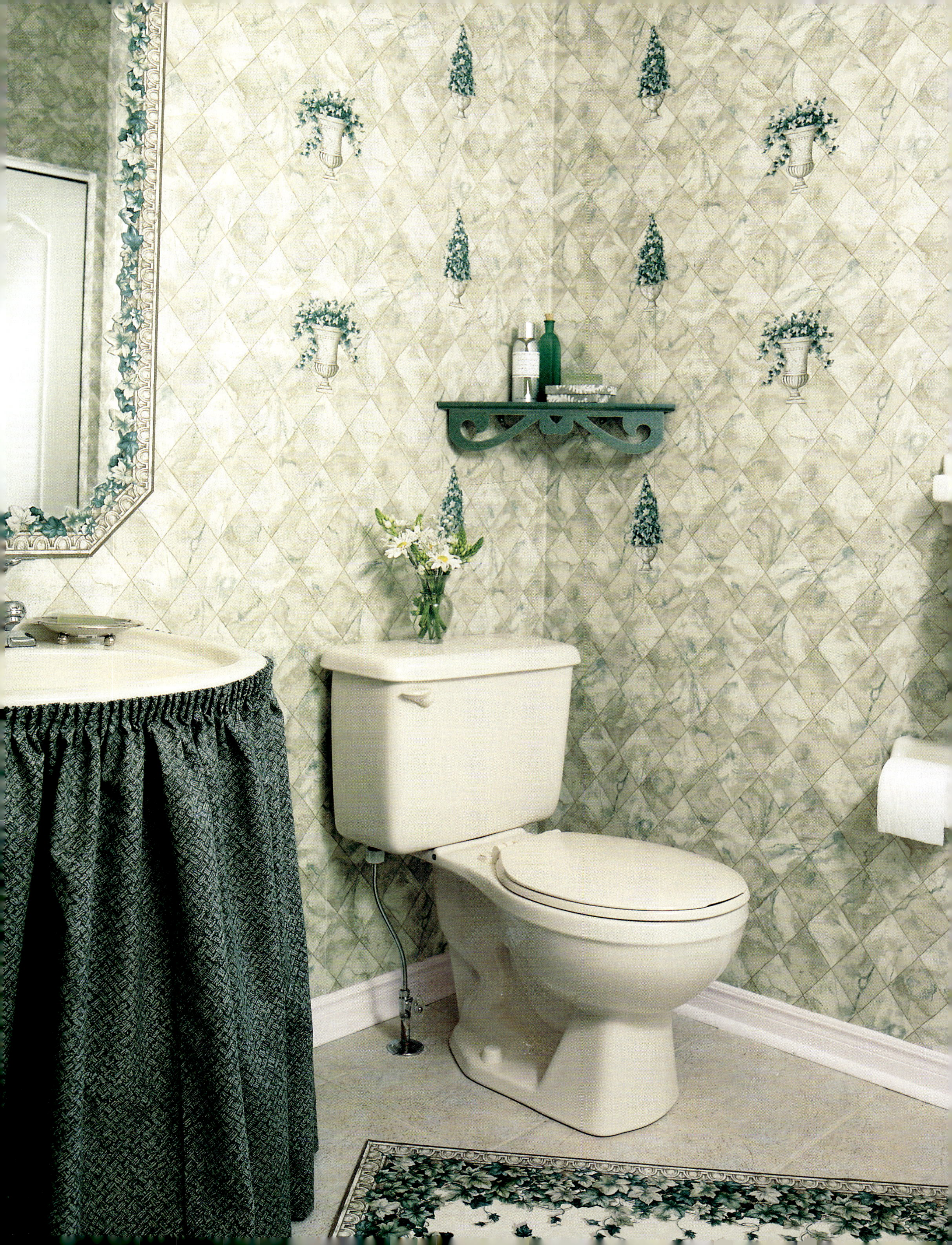

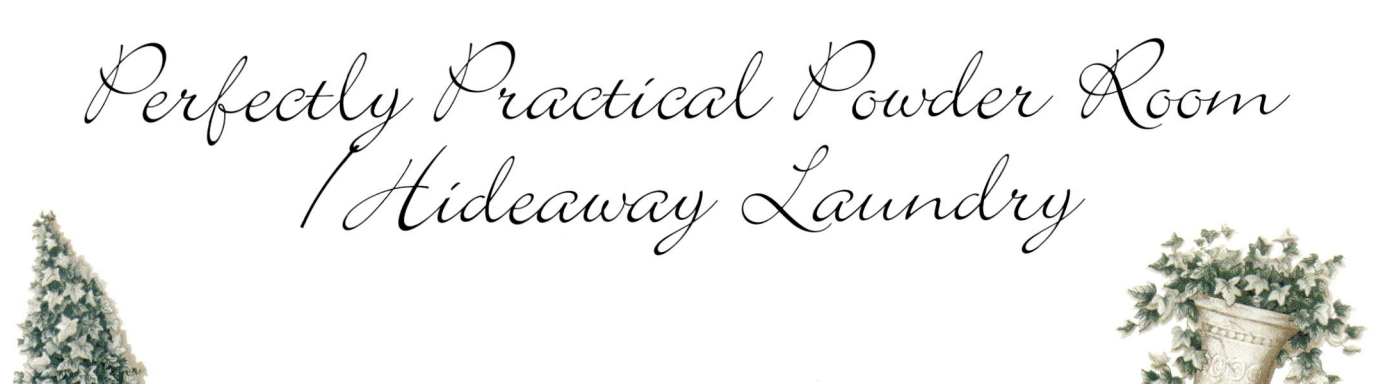

Perfectly Practical Powder Room / Hideaway Laundry

The combined powder room/laundry, located at the end of the entrance hall, does double-duty work in style. Topiary cut-outs from a border customize the subtle harlequin-pattern wallcovering. A delicate coordinating pattern brightens the ceiling. Ivy snipped from a die-cut border rims the mirror and frames the floor mat. The basic sink gets prettied-up with a party-dress treatment made of coordinating fabric attached with Velcro. Folding doors conceal the washer and dryer at the opposite end of the room.

Coordinated durable vinyl-coated wallcoverings decorate the powder room. McCall's Home Dec-in-a-Sec™ pattern for the window treatment #8772.

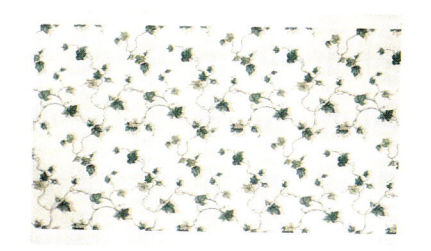

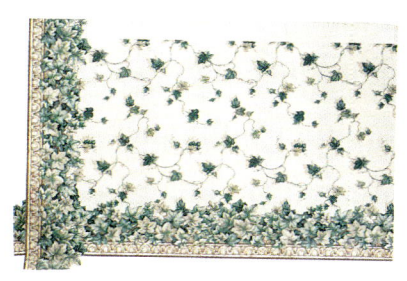

FLOOR SHOW

Create a fanciful mat with Masonite and wallcovering.

SUPPLIES:
- *Masonite, approximately three feet long and no wider than the width of the wallcovering plus twice the width of the border covering*
- *oil-base primer*
- *paintbrush*
- *wallcovering and wallcovering border*
- *high-gloss urethane*

METHOD:

1. Apply oil-base primer to both sides of the Masonite. Let dry.

2. Cut a strip of wallcovering the length of the Masonite board.

3. Following the basic instructions for hanging wallcoverings, apply the strip along the center of the board. Let dry.

4. Following the basic instructions for hanging borders, apply the border around the four edges, mitering the corners as directed on page 39. The outer edges of the border should meet the edge of the board exactly: do not wrap around to the underside. Let dry.

5. Apply at least four coats of urethane, allowing to dry between coats.

WISE ADVICE FROM THE PROS

- Save extra wallcovering for minor repairs, for covering electrical plates or for special decorative projects to accessorize the room.

- To repair a tear, place a larger piece of pasted wallcovering over the tear so that it makes an exact match with the pattern of the wallcovering. Using a razor knife, cut through both layers. Remove the excess on both layers, clean the exposed wall area and repaste the new center piece in the area. After 15 minutes, lightly seam-roll the edges of the fitted piece.

- To reglue loose edges, pull away enough of the strip to apply a thin coat of the correct adhesive underneath. Press down firmly for a few minutes, smooth out air bubbles and wipe off excess adhesive with a damp sponge.

A tailored window treatment adds a charming touch to the small-scale window in the main floor powder room.

Perfectly Practical Powder Room/Hideaway Laundry

BEFORE

Coordinating durable vinyl-coated wallcoverings beautify the bedroom; coordinating fabrics decorate the bed and window areas. McCall's Home Dec-in-a-Sec™ pattern for the tab-top window treatment #8211; McCall's Creative Decor pattern for the duvet and bedskirt #8606; McCall's Home Decorating patterns for the cushions #8081, #8661, #9260 and window seat #9160.

Romantic Retreat

Clusters of roses forming heart-shaped patterns and snippets of poetry written in gold make the master bedroom a romantic retreat. A coordinating die-cut border at ceiling height finishes the room with a flourish. A coordinating wallcovering in the alcove creates a room-within-a-room effect. This pattern reappears on the ceiling above the window seat. Matching fabrics fashion the bedcoverings and cushioned window seat; fabric used for the bedskirt trims the sheer tab-top curtains.

SCREEN GEM

A versatile screen adds dimension to many rooms.

SUPPLIES:
- *premade wooden folding screen (or make one yourself, using particleboard or plywood; panels should not exceed 20 inches in width)*
- *oil-base primer*
- *size*
- *paintbrush*
- *wallcovering*
- *decorative trim, ribbon, flowers, etc.*
- *white craft glue (optional)*

METHOD:
1. Disassemble the screen, so that each panel can be worked on individually. Apply primer, let dry, then apply size. Let dry.

2. Decide where the pattern of your wallcovering will be located on each panel. Cut out a strip, run it through the water trough and apply it to the panel. Wrap it around to the back side of the panel, slitting corners so the wallcovering will lie flat on the

BEFORE

The Well-Dressed Home 62

back. Lay the panel down. Then, determine how to cut the wallcovering for the second panel so that it will match up well with the first. Apply in the same way as the first panel. Repeat until all panels are covered.

3. Apply wallcovering to the back of each panel, trimming the wallcovering flush with the edges of the panels and overlapping the wallcovering that wrapped around from the front. You may need to apply vinyl-to-vinyl adhesive in order for the overlapping wallcovering to adhere firmly. Wipe off excess adhesive and let dry. Apply a coordinating border, if desired, or attach decorative trims.

4. Reassemble the panels.

PICTURE-PERFECT MATTS

Frame your favorite photos with wallcovering matts.

SUPPLIES:
- *picture frames with stiff matts*
- *wallcovering*
- *pencil*
- *razor knife*
- *straight edge*
- *white craft glue*

METHOD:
1. Remove matt from the frame.
2. **Option 1** Lay the matt on the underside of the wallcovering and trace around it. Using a razor knife and straight edge, cut out as drawn. Lay the wallcovering on top of the matt and check that it fits exactly. You may need to remove a thin piece from the inner edge, if the matt has a sloped edge.

   Spread glue evenly over the matt. Press on wallcovering, smoothing out any air bubbles. Set aside to dry. Then, reassemble frame.

3. **Option 2** Cut four strips of wallcovering or border the width of the matt border.

   Spread glue evenly over matt. Lay strips on the matt, overlapping at the corners. Using a razor knife and straight edge, miter the corners (*see Glossary*), cutting through both layers. Lift up the corners and remove the excess pieces of wallcovering. Press the covering back in place, smoothing the joins together. Set aside to dry. Then, reassemble.

4. **Option 3** Cut out motifs from the wallcovering. Spread glue thinly on the underside of pieces and attach to the existing matt.

BEAUTIFUL BOXES

Bring boxes out of the closet: match them to your walls.

SUPPLIES:
- *wallcovering*
- *white craft glue*
- *scissors*
- *decorative trim*
- *very stiff round boxes or hatboxes*

METHOD:
1. Cut out a piece of wallcovering so that it will wrap around the sides of the box bottom and overhang top and bottom edges by one inch. Set aside. Trace around the box bottom on the underside of the wallcovering. Cut out, allowing an extra inch on all sides. Set aside. Repeat for the box top.

2. If you are using a round box, make the top and bottom pieces of wallcovering fit perfectly by cutting slits every half-inch into the edges, ending at the outlines of the box top or bottom. Spread glue evenly over the underside of the top piece. Press in place on box top. Smooth the edges in place, overlapping wallcovering where slits were cut. Let dry. Repeat for the bottom of the box. Let dry.

3. Spread glue evenly over the underside of the wallcovering cut for the side of the box. Press in place. Let dry. Cut a piece of wallcovering to fit the side of the box top. Glue and press in place. Decorate with ribbon, trims, etc.

Romantic Retreat 63

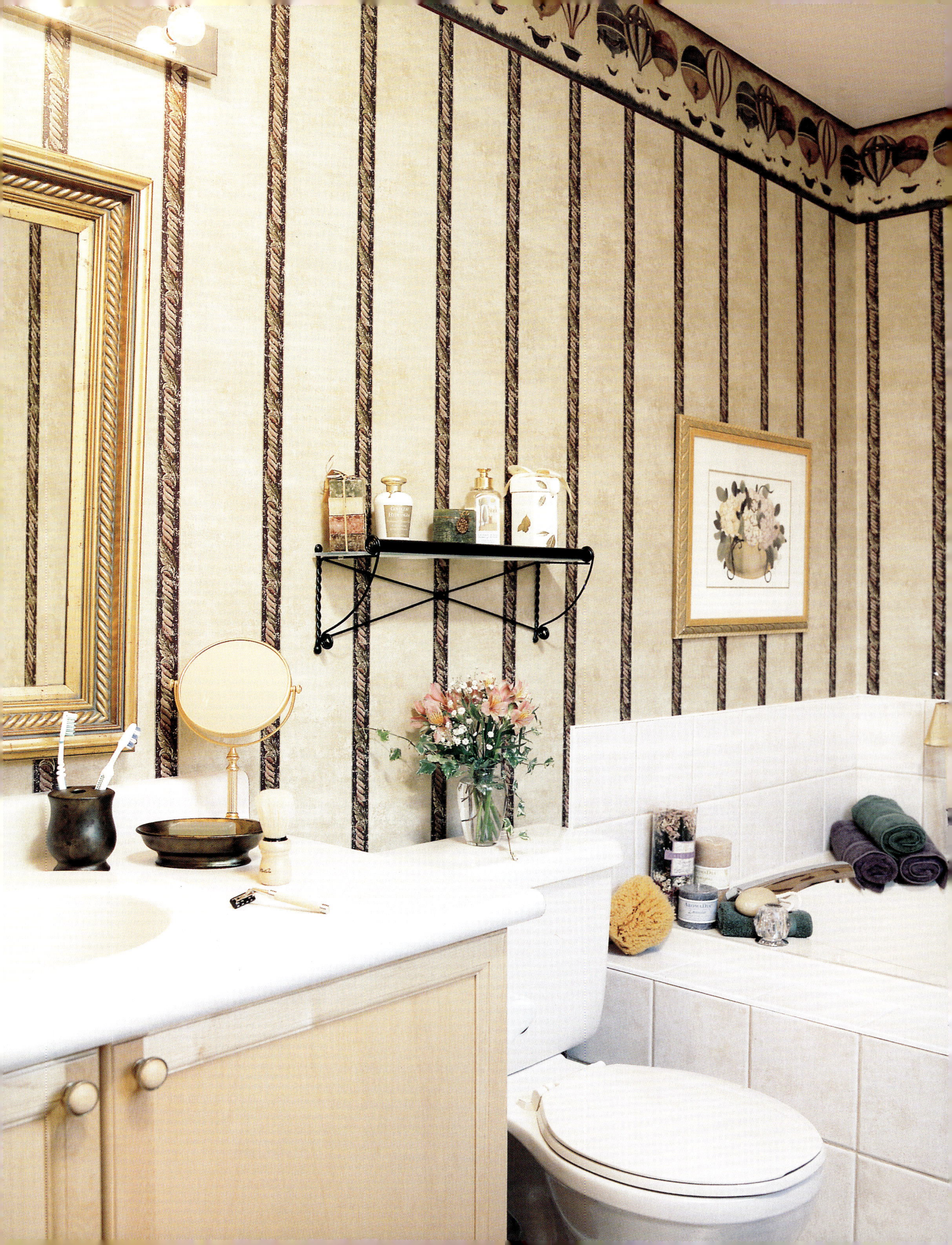

Suite Retreat

Continuing the color scheme from the bedroom, a striped wallcovering banded by a whimsical border of hot-air balloons puts some punch into the basic master bath. The wine-colored rope and acanthus-leaf stripe stands out against a soothing sponge-effect background. The modest window treatment and shower curtain (not shown) borrow fabric from the bedroom. Towels match colors in the wallcoverings.

All the wallcoverings and fabrics in the two rooms forming the master suite are gathered together in one sample book, making the coordination of multiple patterns an easy project.

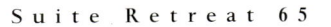

BEFORE

The master bathroom features a durable vinyl-coated wallcovering and border. McCall's Home Dec-in-a-Sec™ pattern for the window treatment #9159.

Suite Retreat 65

BEFORE

Coordinated solid vinyl wallcoverings and borders create the paneled look in the den.

The Well-Dressed Home 66

Double-Duty Den

Striking motifs depicted in calm colors create an elegant guest room/den. Anchored by a futon and desk, the room's charm comes from the ingenious and creative use of three borders and three wallcoverings to produce a paneled look. Injecting a note of playfulness into an otherwise sophisticated room, a fourth bookshelf border and wood trim transform a standard sliding door into a faux library.

McCall's Home Dec-in-a-Sec™ pattern for the window treatment #9259.

Double-Duty Den 67

BEFORE

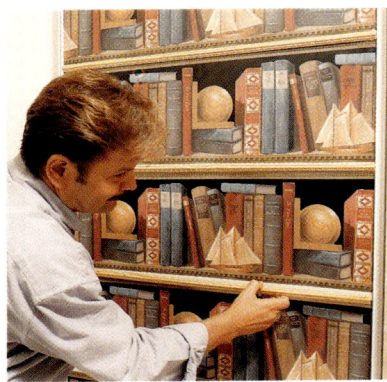

CUSTOMIZE CLOSET DOORS

Create a fool-the-eye library.

SUPPLIES:
- *oil-base primer*
- *level (optional)*
- *metal straight edge*
- *matt-finish urethane*
- *two-inch paintbrush*
- *wood trim (optional)*
- *wallcovering or wallcovering border*
- *size*
- *sponge*

METHOD:
1. Wash doors well and let dry. Be sure to remove all dirt, nails, etc.
2. Apply primer and let dry. Then, apply size, following manufacturer's instructions. Let dry.
3. To create a faux bookshelf, use a level and metal straight edge to draw a horizontal line below the top edge of the door the exact width of the border. (This will be where you will locate the bottom edge of the first row of the border.) Continue to draw horizontal lines across the door at intervals that measure the same as the width of the border plus the width of the wood trim, if using.
4. Cut strips from the border in lengths that are the same as the width of the door. (Do not cut through the books' "spines," if possible, and be sure that there is a variation in the location of books!)
5. Following the directions on the package, attach the strips to the door, beginning at the top. Trim the edges of the wallcovering so they are flush with the edges of the door. Use a wet sponge to rinse off any excess paste. Let dry.
6. Apply two or three coats of urethane. Let dry between coats.
7. For a more authentic look, glue wood trim around the edges of the door and at each shelf level.

CREATE A PANEL-LOOK WALL

Panels can be hung on any walls in whatever sizes are appropriate to the room.

SUPPLIES:
- *several wallcoverings*
- *pencil*
- *straight edge*
- *razor knife*
- *vinyl-to-vinyl adhesive (optional)*

METHOD:
1. Hang wallcovering on one wall at a time. Determine where the panels are to be located on that wall and mark their corners with a pencil. Make sure that all panels are spaced an equal distance apart and at the same height.
2. Cut out the panel covering as close to the finished size as possible. (It is better to cut it too large, rather than too small.)
3. Wet the covering and apply it to the wall where marked with the pencil.
4. Using a metal straight edge and razor knife to trim around the edges of each panel, cut through the base covering. Peel off the panel piece and set it aside. Peel the base wallcovering off the wall; insert the panel back into this bare spot.
5. As an alternative to cutting out the base covering, you can apply vinyl-to-vinyl adhesive on the underside of the panel pieces and attach them directly to the base wallcovering. While this is an easier method, the panel will not sit flush with the base wallcovering.
6. Apply the border around the panel, using vinyl-to-vinyl adhesive. Position the border so that it hides the seams where the panels join the base wallcovering. Miter the corners, as directed on page 39. Wipe off excess paste.

Double-Duty Den 69

BEFORE

Various vinyl-coated and solid vinyl wallcoverings and die-cut borders transform the basic room into a secret garden; coordinating fabrics brighten the bed and windows.

The Well-Dressed Home 70

The Secret Garden

This fantasy bedroom for a little girl proves that you don't have to be an artist to create a mural when you can use wallcoverings to achieve the same effect. As long as you can cut and paste, you can make a mural with little effort. Start with a clear idea of what you want to create. Make a rough sketch on a piece of paper. Then, select wallcoverings that will give you the look you want. Don't limit yourself to one wallcovering collection or book: search through several books, in-store designs and even clearance bins.

Apply the background wallcovering first and build your design elements on top, according to your original sketch. Cut out shapes and apply as you would if you were doing découpage, using vinyl-to-vinyl adhesive. Wipe away excess adhesive as you proceed.

Then, to complete the fantasy, sew bedcoverings and window treatments, using coordinating fabrics.

The Secret Garden 71

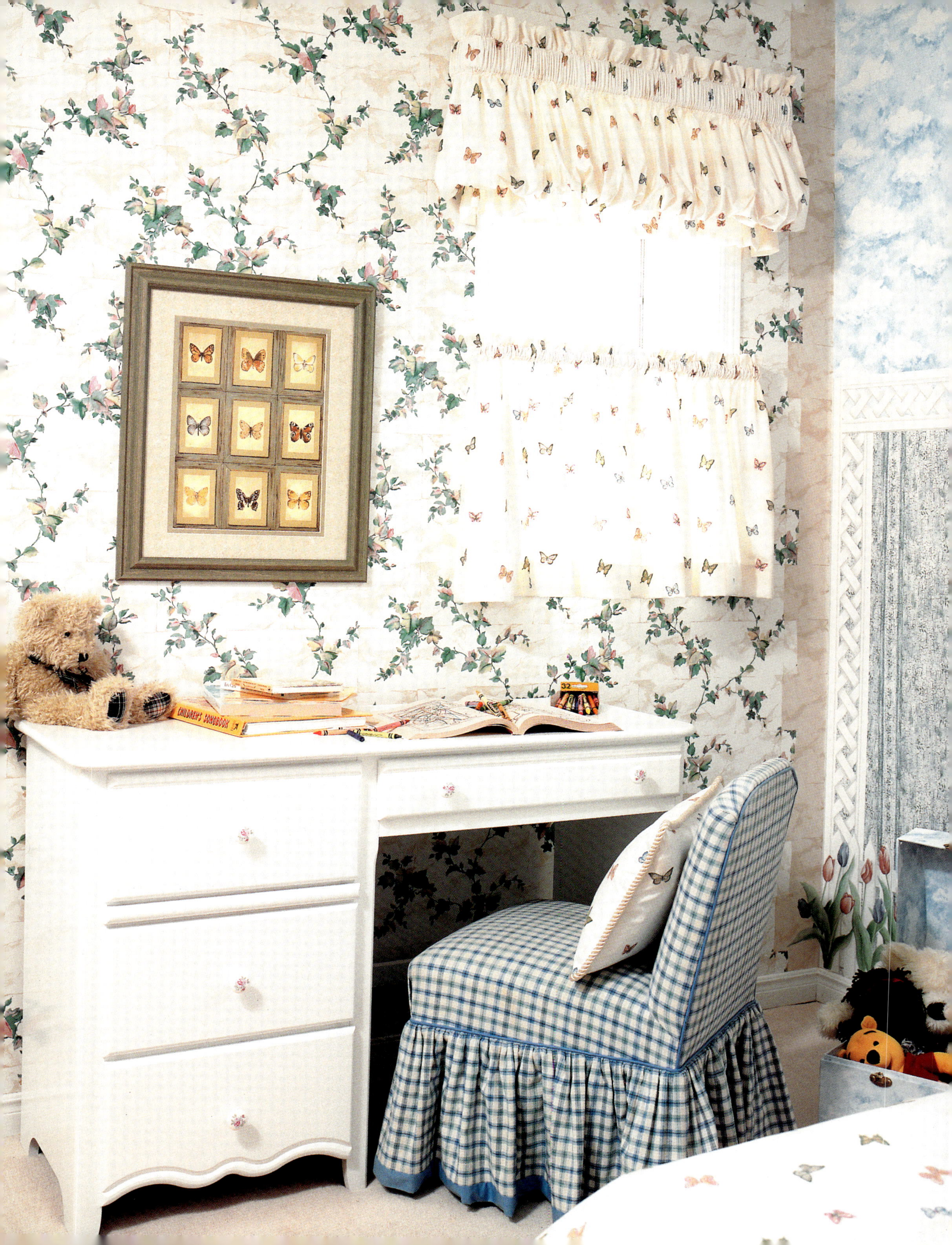
CHILDREN'S SONGBOOK
32

Create a fence-look by cutting strips of wallcovering.

Lattice borders are joined to create the headboard.

Flowers are cut out of a coordinating border to add dimension to the headboard.

McCall's Home Decorating pattern for the window treatment #7486 and cushions #8081 and #8661. McCall's Creative Decor pattern for the duvet, bedskirt and pillow shams #8606.

CREATE A CLOUD-COVERED TOY BOX

Use wallcovering to transform a toy box into a work of art. Be sure the chest is clean and dust-free. Sand any bumps. Cut the wallcovering into pieces to fit all surfaces. Dip the pieces in water and press firmly to the box. Be sure to cut the side pieces long enough to fold them over to the inside along the top edges. Cover the inside of the chest last. Let dry. Then, apply two or three coats of urethane over the entire box.

WISE ADVICE FROM THE PROS

- Use the proper smoother. Different papers require different smoothing tools. Using the correct one will make the job easier and protect the wallcovering from damage when it is being applied.

The Secret Garden 73

Durable vinyl-coated wallcoverings decorate the bathroom.

Refreshing and Relaxing Bath

Branches of pretty pastel magnolias trail across the lively floral wallcovering of the main bathroom. A coordinating stripe draws the eye to the ceiling and away from the standard plumbing fixtures in this long narrow room. A modest window treatment sewn from coordinating fabrics suits the small opening. Towels and tub accessories tie in with the color of the magnolia leaves.

BEFORE

McCall's Home Dec-in-a-Sec™ pattern for the window treatment #8211.

More Decorating Ideas Using Wallcoverings

PAINTABLE WALLCOVERINGS PROVIDE MANY EXCITING OPTIONS

After hanging paintable wallcoverings, consider these decorating options:

1. Use a rag or wad of cheesecloth to wipe paint on the surface. This will coat only the surface of the design with color, leaving the crevices and indentations white. (See inside front cover photo.)

2. Use a paint roller to apply paint. Then, use a rag to wipe the paint off the surface. This will coat the crevices and indentations with color, leaving only a faint tint of paint on the raised surface design. (See inside back cover photo.)

3. Use a paint roller to apply paint, covering the entire surface. Apply a second coat of paint in the same way. This will give a solid coat of color, with the overall pattern providing texture.

4. Use more than one color of paint for these techniques to create a faux-stone or sponged look.

Unfinished

Painted

FANCIED-UP FURNITURE

Any furniture can be fancied up with wallcovering, as long as it is well protected with urethane. Just cut motifs from wallcovering and apply to furniture, using vinyl adhesive. Wipe off excess adhesive and set aside to dry. Apply four to six coats of urethane, allowing to dry between coats.

If the furniture is to be completely covered with wallcovering, cut out pieces specifically for each section of the piece. Match patterns carefully. Use vinyl wallcovering adhesive to attach the covering. Wipe away any excess. Apply six coats of urethane.

COVER UP A BOX

Set decorative boxes on a table or shelf.

SUPPLIES:
- *heavy box with separate lid*
- *wallcovering*
- *ruler and pencil*
- *white craft glue*
- *trims (optional)*

METHOD:

1. Lay wallcovering wrong-side up on a table. Set the box bottom in the center. Lift the covering up the side and end edges and mark where it reaches the top. Add one inch and, using a ruler, draw a rectangular shape this size on the underside of the wallcovering. Cut it out.

2. Place the box bottom in the center of the piece of wallcovering and draw around its base. Use the ruler to extend the lines out to the edges. You will have a large rectangle in the center and four small rectangles in each corner.

3. Cut out the small corner squares, leaving a half-inch additional allowance on the inner sides. Cut a miter slit into each corner, ending the slit at the place marked on the wallcovering where the bottom of the box will sit.

4. Press under the extra allowances of the end pieces. Return the box bottom to its place on the wrong side of the wallcovering. Spread a thin line of glue along the upper and end edges of the two side pieces of covering. Lift up the side pieces and fold the glued edges to the inside of the top rim of the box; press the glued end edges around to the ends of the box.

5. Spread a thin line of glue along the top edges of the end pieces of wallcovering and along the folded-in edges of extra allowance. Lift the covering up and over the top rim of the box and press in place inside the rim and along the outside ends.

6. Cover the lid the same way.

DO-IT-YOURSELF DECORATIVE ACCESSORIES

Match the decor in any room with designer-bright decorative accessories. Take a look at some of the possibilities for quick-to-do wallcovering projects. Look around your house for more ideas. Use wallcoverings to:

Decorate a flower box with coordinating wallcovering.

- customize canister sets in the kitchen
- coordinate desk sets in a home office, including desk pad, file organizers, magazine holders, pen and pencil containers
- pretty-up photo-album and scrapbook covers
- add glamor to drawer liners and closet shelves
- provide an edging for open cupboard shelves (die-cut borders are great for this)
- freshen up panels on old doors
- add a decorative border on a window blind
- fancy up a flower box
- cover a tissue dispenser, wastebasket and other accessories in a bathroom
- decorate a mirror frame

Almost everything can be covered with wallcovering to create coordinating decorative accessories. To protect the covering, apply two or more coats of urethane after the project is completed. Do not attempt to cover objects that will be in frequent contact with water.

More Decorating Ideas Using Wallcoverings

Glossary

ACCORDION FOLDING
The technique of "booking" (see below) a strip of wallcovering or border several times, resembling an accordion. This keeps pasted sides together, allows "relaxing" time and makes long strips easier to handle during installation.

ADHESIVE
A substance that causes one thing to adhere to another. Most wallcovering adhesives are cellulose-, clay- or starch-based.

ALLOWANCE
The extra amount of wallcovering allowed at the top, bottom and/or sides of a strip that is trimmed off after the strip is placed on the wall.

BOOKING
It is necessary to book prepasted wallcovering after it has been immersed in water to ensure that all the paste is activated and to help prevent the seams from shrinking once the wallcovering is on the wall. To "book" a strip of prepasted wallcovering, lift it from the water and lay it paste-side up on a flat surface. Fold the top half to the middle of the sheet, paste-to-paste, and the bottom to the middle, paste-to-paste, being careful not to crease the edges. Leave for about three minutes.

BORDER
A narrow band of wallcovering used for decorative purposes, usually at ceiling height, as a chair-rail detail or around windows and doors.

BUTT JOINT/BUTTED SEAM
A joint at which edges of wallcovering meet but do not overlap.

DROP MATCH
See page 31.

DYE-LOT NUMBER
A set of numbers and/or letters given to a particular batch of wallcovering rolls printed at the same time. Each time a new ink or different batch is printed, the dye-lot number (sometimes called the color-run number) will change. It is important to ensure that all rolls have the same dye-lot number before beginning a job.

INSIDE CORNER
A corner that does not protrude into a room.

LEVEL
A four-foot carpenter's level is useful for determining the straightness of seams and the horizontal line of borders. A liquid in a small glass cylinder moves to indicate when it is positioned perfectly level.

LINING PAPER
Lining paper is blank wallcovering stock, which can be applied to prepped walls. It maximizes adhesion, provides a smooth surface and minimizes the possibility of mildew and staining. There are many types, including canvas, strippable, prepasted

and super-heavyweight. It is often recommended for hanging foil, mylar, unbacked fabric and grasscloth coverings. It is hung horizontally (using the same adhesive as the wallcovering), thus ensuring that the seams of the lining paper and the wallcovering do not fall on the same vertical line. It should be left to dry on the wall for at least 36 hours before wallcovering is applied. Super-heavyweight strippable lining paper can be used directly over properly primed and prepared paneling, tile and cement block.

MITER
A cut angled at 45 degrees made where two pieces of border meet and change directions.

OUTSIDE CORNER
A corner that protrudes into a room.

PATTERN REPEAT
See page 30.

PLUMB LINE
A length of string usually coated with chalk to which a weight is attached. It provides a vertical guideline; when the string is snapped, the chalk leaves a mark on the wall.

PREPASTED WALLCOVERING
Wallcovering that has been coated with adhesive during manufacture. The dry adhesive is activated by soaking the covering in water for a specified length of time.

PRIMER/SEALER
A base coating designed for use under wallcovering to seal porous surfaces prior to hanging. A wallcovering primer/sealer helps the wallcovering adhere by blocking the wall's capacity to absorb moisture from the paste. Use either an oil-based primer or a high-quality latex primer.

PUCKERS
Air bubbles that may be removed by a small razor-blade cut, allowing the air to escape.

RANDOM MATCH
See page 30.

RAZOR KNIFE
A long sharp blade that can be kept continuously sharp by snapping off dull ends, leaving a new point. Useful for trimming wallcoverings at ceilings and baseboards and for trimming through wallcovering layers.

SEAM ROLLER
A small narrow roller made from plastic, nylon or wood, that, when pressed along seam joins, presses wallcovering securely to the wall.

SIZE
An inexpensive, easy-to-apply and quick-drying compound applied to the porous surface of a wall to seal it before hanging a wallcovering. It also helps you to move the wallcovering while it's being applied and makes it easier to remove at a later date.

SMOOTHING BRUSH
Depending on the type of wallcovering being applied, a brush, felt-lined plastic handle or plastic triangle tool is used to gently smooth the wallcovering against the wall.

SPACKLING COMPOUND
A white powder to which water is added for use in mending cracks in plaster or filling holes in walls. It should be sanded smooth and flat after drying.

STRAIGHT EDGE
Metal rulers or straight edges are helpful in conjunction with a razor knife for mitering straight and corner joins and for trimming wallcoverings.

STRAIGHT MATCH
See page 30.

WATER TRAY
A specially shaped trough, usually made of plastic, designed to hold water for soaking prepasted wallcoverings before hanging.

WORK TABLE
For ease in cutting and gluing wallcoverings, a work table is invaluable.

VINYL-TO-VINYL ADHESIVE
When hanging wallcovering borders or joining wallcoverings, the use of special adhesive is recommended to make sure the two coverings stick together well. Check manufacturer's suggestions on the appropriate vinyl-to-vinyl adhesive to use.

Index

Borders *38, 39*
Color schemes *20, 22, 23*
Color theory *13, 15, 16*
Decorating plan *19, 20*
Design tips *16*
Dye lots *30*
Loose edges *58*
Pattern-match repeats *30, 31*
Project:
    Boxes *63, 76*
    Closet doors *68*
    Electrical plates *46*
    Floor mat *58*
    Lamp shade *51*
    Panel-look walls *69*
    Picture matts *63*
    Pillars *50*
    Screen *62*
    Tiles *54*
    Toy box *73*
    Window valance *50*
Puckers (air pockets) *39*
Repair
    Loose edges *58*
    Tears *58*
Wall preparation *33, 34*
    New walls *33*
    Previously painted walls *33*
    Previously wallcovered walls *33*
Wallcovering:
    Cleaning *27*
    History of *9, 10, 11*
    How to hang *35*
    • on walls *36*
    • on ceilings *37*
    • borders *38, 39*
    Patterns *30, 31*
    Quantities: how to calculate *28, 29*
    Removal of *25, 26, 27*
    Types *25*
        Bridging materials *27*
        Expanded vinyl/paintable *26*
        Fabric-backed vinyl *26*
        In-register paper-backed vinyl *26*
        Natural fibers *26*
        Paper-backed vinyl *25*
        Solid vinyl *25*
        Strippable vinyl coat *25*

Sources

In the "before" photographs, all furniture is from *Sears Whole Home Stores*; all lamps, framed prints, throws and the table in the den are from *B.B. Bargoon's*.

ENTRANCE
Bench, carpet, *Sears Whole Home Stores*. Blue cushion, *Sears Canada*. All other cushions, *Suzanne Davison Interior Designs Inc*. Framed print, *B.B. Bargoon's*.

LIVING ROOM
Sofas, plaid chair, chest, coffee table, plant stand, *Sears Whole Home Stores*. Potpourri bowl, blue cushion, *Sears Canada*. Bergère chair, matching footstool, ceramic garden stool, *Suzanne Davison Interior Designs Inc*. Framed prints, lamps, *B.B. Bargoon's*.

DINING ROOM
Buffet, table, chairs, tableware, *Sears Whole Home Stores*. Candlesticks, *Sears Canada*. Mirror, *Ginger's Bath Centre*.

KITCHEN
Table, chairs, *Sears Whole Home Stores*. Carpet, tableware, colander, appliances, kettle, *Sears Canada*. Framed print, *B.B. Bargoon's*.

POWDER ROOM/LAUNDRY
Towels, *Sears Canada*. Accessories on shelf, *Ginger's Bath Centre*.

MASTER BEDROOM
Bed, chests of drawers, chairs, *Sears Whole Home Stores*. Bed tray, cup and saucer, *Sears Canada*. Lamps, framed prints, *B.B. Bargoon's*. Robe, *Ginger's Bath Centre*.

MASTER BATHROOM
Towels, mirror, shaving mirror, gold lamp shade, soaps, sponge, accessories on shelf, *Ginger's Bath Centre*. Framed print, *B.B. Bargoon's*. Aromatherapy candles, potpourri, *Sears Canada*.

DEN
Desk, chair, futon, *Sears Whole Home Stores*. Leopard-print cushion, wastebasket, *Sears Canada*. Framed prints, lamp, all other cushions, *B.B. Bargoon's*.

THE SECRET GARDEN
Bed, chest of drawers, desk, *Sears Whole Home Stores*. Sheets, *Sears Canada*. Lamp, framed print, *B.B. Bargoon's*.

MAIN BATHROOM
Towels, bath mat, basket, *Sears Canada*. Neck roll, soaps, soap dispenser, *Ginger's Bath Centre*.

Visit your nearest Sears retail store in the U.S, or Sears Whole Home Furniture store or retail store in Canada.

B.B. Bargoon's, 8201 Keele St., Unit 1, Concord, ON L4K 1Z4 (905) 761-7799

Ginger's Bath Centre, 1275 Castlefield Ave., Toronto, ON M6B 1G4 (416) 787-1787

Suzanne Davison Interior Designs Inc. (416) 481-5254

House built by: Country Homes, 741 Roundtree Dairy Rd, Unit 2, Woodbridge, ON L4L 5T9 (416) 213-7191